SAINT JOSEPH

and

THE INTERIOR LIFE

SAINT JOSEPH

"The husband of Mary, of whom was born Jesus, who is called Christ—being (as was supposed) the son of Joseph"

A SHORT LIFE BASED ON THE GOSPELS

by
HENRY V. GILL, S.J.

A Selection of
SPIRITUAL BOOK ASSOCIATES

printed with the permission of
M. H. GILL AND SON, LTD.
50 UPPER O'CONNELL STREET
DUBLIN

𝔑𝔦𝔥𝔦𝔩 𝔒𝔟𝔰𝔱𝔞𝔱:
    PATRICIUS DARGAN
      Censor Theol. Deput

𝔍𝔪𝔭𝔯𝔦𝔪𝔦 𝔓𝔬𝔱𝔢𝔰𝔱:
    ✠ IOANNES CAROLUS
      ARCHIEP. DUBLINEN.
      Hiberniæ Primas

Dublini, die 24° Novembris, anno 1945

SPIRITUAL BOOK ASSOCIATES
381 FOURTH AVENUE, NEW YORK 16, N. Y.

PRINTED IN THE UNITED STATES OF AMERICA

Dedicated

to

The Virgin Mary

Spouse of St. Joseph

BIOGRAPHICAL NOTE

FATHER HENRY GILL, S.J., the author of this *Life of St. Joseph*, was a well-known writer and lecturer on scientific subjects. The son of the late Mr. H. J. Gill, M.A., J.P., who was for many years a member of the former Irish Parliamentary Party and head of the publishing firm of Messrs. M. H. Gill and Son, Ltd., Father Gill studied Physics for two years at Cambridge under Professor J. J. Thomson, at a time when the Cavendish Laboratory was becoming, under Thomson's direction, a world-famous centre of physical research. Father Gill was keenly interested in modern research into the problems of atomic structure, electricity and seismology. He read some interesting papers before the Royal Society and the Royal Dublin Society, and was also a regular contributor, chiefly on scientific subjects, to *Studies*, *Thought* and the *Irish Ecclesiastical Record*. In the last years of his life he gathered a selection of these various essays into a single volume, which he published under the title *Fact and Fiction in Modern Science* (1943). This volume, though published in the difficult war-years, met with an immediate success in England as well as in Ireland, while an American edition was printed by the University of Fordham in 1945, and an edition in Portuguese will be published shortly by Edicoes Gama, of Lisbon. He also wrote a short life of the celebrated Jesuit scientist, Roger Boscovich, which was published in 1942.

Father Gill was thus well-known in scientific circles, but he was even better known to the wide circle of his

friends as a devout and, at the same time, very human
Catholic priest. During the four long years of the first
World War, Father Gill served as a military chaplain to
the Second Battalion of the Royal Irish Rifles, and was
awarded the M.C. and D.S.O. for his gallant conduct.
He was in the trenches with his regiment, almost without intermission, throughout those four years, and there
are still many of the officers and men of his old regiment
who cherish memories of affectionate gratitude for their
former chaplain. During the last twenty-five years of his
life, Father Gill worked as a Jesuit priest in his native
city of Dublin: as Spiritual Father to the young students
of University Hall; as Minister in Belvedere College and
Rathfarnham Castle; and finally as one of the small community of priests in the Jesuit residence at 35 Lower
Leeson Street. Here he was able to concentrate his at-
tentions on the literary work for which he had always
shown special aptitude, and it was during these last years
that he began to publish articles and books on spiritual
topics which had been, for so many years, a centre of his
own personal interest and study. His first volume of this
kind was published in 1935, under the title *Jesuit Spirit-
uality*; it is a quiet, but very helpful commentary on the
Spiritual Exercises of Saint Ignatius. Five years later he
published a further series of essays on the same general
theme, under the title *Christianity in Daily Life*. During
his last years, when his health was already beginning to
fail, he set himself to prepare a book on the life of Saint
Joseph, to whom he had always shown very special devotion.

In his writings and in private conversation, Father
Gill was insistent that Christian devotion should be cen-

tred round the life and teaching of Our Blessed Lord, Whose Incarnation is in fact the central mystery of our Christian Faith. It will be seen that this short *Life of Saint Joseph* is designed to give the reader a deeper insight into the mysteries of the Hidden Life of Our Lord —that story of Bethlehem and Nazareth that has been for so many centuries a source of consolation and devout joy to Christian souls. Father Gill spent much of the last years of his life in the study of the principal Catholic commentaries on the Four Gospels, and he has gathered the fruit of his long reading and meditation into the pages of this little book. It was his hope that, by telling once more the familiar narrative of St. Matthew and St. Luke in the light of the traditional commentaries of Catholic theologians and scholars, he might help others to share his own deep interest in the sublime mysteries that lie hidden beneath the simple Gospel story.

God gave him strength to see this book through the last stages of proof-correction, and he was still able, though then very feeble, to write in his own hand the final invocation which will be found on the last page: *Saint Joseph, Patron of a Happy Death, pray for us.* Two or three days later the call came quietly and peacefully, whilst the members of his own community were offering the Holy Sacrifice for that grace of a happy Christian death which Saint Joseph has obtained for so many of his clients.

Requiescat in pace!

A. GWYNN, S.J.

FOREWORD

THE object of this little book is not to add another to the many which have been written on the practice of devotion to St. Joseph, but rather as a help to the better understanding of the place of that great Saint in the earthly lives of Jesus and Mary, which is so necessary to solid devotion. All who read the Gospel story carefully must realise that, while the main facts connected with the Incarnation and the Holy Family are stated clearly, there are many details of interest which are either omitted altogether or referred to in a way which gives rise to not a few problems. Such facts would have been known to the contemporaries of the Evangelists and others who lived during or shortly after the time of Christ, but they are not known with certainty to us. These pages are not written from a controversial point of view, but the author can claim to have taken no little trouble to reconstruct a *Life of St. Joseph* with the aid of the Gospels, interpreted according to Galilean customs, by the best available authorities. Since the life of Joseph takes its special importance from his association with Jesus Christ and the Blessed Virgin Mary, these pages might almost as well be looked on as a brief account of the Holy Family. They are, however, after the example of St. Matthew, written from the standpoint of St. Joseph, the "supposed" father of Jesus, rather than from that of Mary, His Virgin-Mother, as in the Gospel of St. Luke. It makes little difference which standpoint is taken, since, in the designs of God, their lives are so interwoven in the story of the coming of Jesus Christ the Son of God into the world, that it is difficult to describe the place of either without including that of the other. But the determining motive for placing the name of St. Joseph at the head of these pages is the desire of offering them as an expression of gratitude—however inadequate—for many favours obtained through his intercession.

In compiling this little volume I have made use of the well-known modern works on the Life of Christ as well as the standard Commentaries. For a fuller treat-ment of many points not dealt with in the modern lives of Christ the reader is referred to the *De Mysteriis Vitæ Christi* of Suarez, and the *Commentarii de SS. Corde Jesu, de Beata Virgine Maria et de S. Josepho Sponso B. Mariæ V.*, by P. Januarius Bucceroni, S.J. (Ed. iv, Rome, 1896), as well as the recognised treatises on the Incarnation. More easily available by the general reader, and containing a mine of interesting information on the manner of life of the Jewish people, is a series of articles—unfortunately not published in book-form—by Fr. E. Power, S.J., D.Litt. Orient., Prof. of Biblical Archæology, Biblical Institute, Rome, in *Studies* (Vols. VIII, IX, X, 1919-1921), on *Palestinian Customs as illustrating the Bible.*

I have deliberately refrained from introducing any mention of the many traditions—and legends—which have grown up around St. Joseph and the Holy Family, except those which have received some recognition by the Church, such as a commemoration in her Liturgy.

Feast of the Visitation, 1945.

CONTENTS

CONTENTS

SAINT JOSEPH

CHAPTER I

THE BIRTH AND EARLY LIFE OF MARY

"The name of the Virgin was Mary."—(Luke i, 27)

IN all literature no story in history or fiction has ever approached in beauty and human interest the Gospel narrative of the coming of Jesus Christ into the world. In it the natural and supernatural are so blended that each supplements and sheds lustre on the other, to present a story which depicts all that is purest and noblest in human nature. In this story the opening phrases centre round Mary, the Virgin Mother of Jesus, and Joseph, who was looked on by men to be His earthly father in the ordinary human way.

The lives of Mary and Joseph are so inseparably interwoven that it is impossible to understand fully the part of either in the working out of the divine plan of the Incarnation without including that of the other. The life of Mary takes its supreme importance from her virgin motherhood of the Son of God, while that of Joseph takes it from his association with her as her husband appointed by God to be the head of the Holy Family and the legal father of Jesus, through whom He was to be accepted by men as the Son of David and the Messiah. The Gospel of St. Luke centres round Mary, and tells the story as it came from her own lips. That of St. Matthew makes Joseph the central figure, but both agree in joining together Jesus, Mary and Joseph, these three so dear to God and to every Christian.

The chief source of our knowledge of all that concerns the birth and early life of Christ must always be the Gospels, and they tell us all that it is essential for us to know. There are, however, many details which we should like to understand more fully, but about which the Scriptures are silent, and which can only be gathered from a close examination of the text of the Bible in the light of the information we possess of the customs and manner of life of the Jewish people in those far distant days.

To fill in and complete the picture we must have recourse to the early writers and the Fathers of the Church, and to the theologians, concerning the outward circumstances of His birth. Above all, it is necessary to bear in mind that, in the eyes of their contemporaries, Jesus was "supposed to be" the son of Joseph and Mary through ordinary human generation: "And they said: Is not this Jesus the son of Joseph, whose father and mother we know?" (Luke vi, 42); again: "And coming into His own country, he taught them in their synagogues, so they said: How came this man by his wisdom and miracles? Is not this the carpenter's son? Is not his mother called Mary, and his brethren James, and Joseph, and Simon and Jude: and his sisters, are not they all with us?" (Matt. xiii, 54-56).

The secret of the virgin birth was first published to the world by the inspired writers, although it is probable that it was known to some of Christ's followers during His lifetime. From this it follows that the marriage of Mary and Joseph, and the conception and birth of Jesus must have taken place under circumstances which, in the estimation of all, were in every respect honourable and fitted to safeguard the good name of Mary and the honourable parentage of her Son in the eyes of the Jewish people among whom they lived. For any suspicion that Joseph was not the earthly father of Christ in the usual meaning of the word would have cast doubts on the good name of Mary and on the legitimacy of her Son.

The Scripture does not give us any direct information as to the family history of Our Lady. According to the universally accepted tradition, supported by the Masses and Offices prescribed in their honor, Mary was the daughter of Joachim and Anne, descendants of David. According to some authorities she was an only child, given to them in answer to long and fervent prayer and fasting. But nearly all the modern writers hold that she had a sister, named Mary like herself, who was married to Cleophas, a brother of Joseph, and who is referred to in the account of the crucifixion in St. John's Gospel (xix, 25):

"Now there stood by the cross of Jesus His mother, and His mother's sister, Mary of Cleophas, and Mary Magdalen."

The view that Cleophas—or Alpheus [1]—was the brother of Joseph is sufficient to account for their children being called the brothers and sisters of Jesus. The parents of Mary are spoken of as being of a fairly prosperous condition of life, and Our Lady herself as heiress to their property and owner of the Holy House.

The place of Mary's birth is not stated in the Gospels. Tradition is divided between the neighbourhood of Jerusalem and Nazareth. In any case, we know that the Annunciation took place at Nazareth, and the fact that her relatives belonged to this region is an argument in favour of the latter view. I think that all of us would like to be able to think that the mother of Jesus was born in Galilee, and that this was Jesus' "own country," not only because His own homeland was full of happy memories and the scene of the most fruitful years of His missionary labours, but also because it was the native place of His beloved mother.

In working out the plan of the Redemption, God selected the times, places and conditions which were in harmony with the human as well as the supernatural objects He had in view. The contrast between the peaceful life of Jesus at Nazareth with Mary and Joseph, and His death on the cross, beneath which His mother stood at Jerusalem, corresponds to the difference between the physical aspects of the two places. Writing of Jerusalem, a modern writer gives the following description of the effect its appearance has on the Christian mind:

---

[1] These two names, though apparently different, represent two ways of pronouncing the same Aramaic name; one form with the aspirate, and the other without it.

"My first thought was amazement that Jerusalem should ever have been built. A more unlikely place for a famous city cannot be imagined. The arid mountains lie about it (the city is 2,600 feet above sea level) rolling in long brown ridges against the sky . . .

"My second thought was that never had I seen a more intolerant looking city. All the hardness of the rock and the smouldering fires within the rock seemed to have boiled up out of the bowels of the earth and cooled into the city of Jerusalem. It was a perfect expression, so it seemed to me, of the cruelty and fierceness of the Judean highlands. This high city, perched above ravines and lying among the debris of centuries, might, it seemed, be the abode not of men and women and children, but the dwelling-place of ruthless emotions such as Pride and Arrogance and Hate. As I sat for a long time looking down on Jerusalem, I thought to myself: 'That is undoubtedly the place that crucified Jesus Christ.' Like an echo to my thought came the terrible reply: 'And it would probably do so again.'

"The longer I looked at Jerusalem the more I felt convinced that my first impression was not overdrawn or extravagant. If Jerusalem has not been born out of volcanic lava, she has at least been born from the fire of men's minds. Splendid and terrible things have happened behind her walls. The modern world was born in their shadow. Strange that the greatest event in the history of mankind should have occurred on this bare plateau; stranger still, perhaps, that Jerusalem should still wear her air of intolerance. I seemed to hear a Voice in the pulse of the heat, and the Voice said: 'Jerusalem, Jerusalem, thou that killest the prophets, and stonest them that are sent unto thee, how often would I have gathered together thy children, as the hen doth gather her chickens under her wings, and thou wouldst not!' The words beat against my brain like an echo of the heat that quivered above the Mount of Olives. I listened again, but there was no sound but the thrusting of the plough through the dry soil and the click of a mule's hoof against a flint." [2]

Galilee, on the other hand, is described by all writers, ancient as well as modern, as a beautiful and fruitful region, abounding in all that can satisfy the eye and contribute to the needs of human life. It was a land of fertile plains and pasture lands, of streams running through valleys between gentle hills covered with wild flowers, sloping down towards the Mediterranean on the west and to the Sea of Galilee on the east. Nazareth is thus described by Fouard:

"Nazareth belongs to Galilee, and nestles down along the mountain-side, shielded from the plain of Esdraelon by the many hill-tops which are crossed by those winding foot-paths and steep, hilly roads. On the confines of the village these crests stand apart for a space (as it were), so as to encircle it with their wooded heights and grassy vale. Some scholars have presumed that this verdant amphitheatre was once the crater of an extinct volcano, and indeed the fertility of

[2] *In the Steps of the Master*, H. V. Morton, Ch. i, 5.

the spot supports this conjecture. In fact, Palestine has no more smiling glades than this little valley of Nazareth. Antonius the Martyr compares it to a paradise. 'Its women are of an incomparable grace,' he says, 'and their beauty, which surpasses that of all the maidens of Juda, is a gift from Mary. As for its wines, its honey, its oil and its fruits, it yields not the palm even to fruitful Egypt." [3]

When a maiden arrived at marriageable age—which was about fourteen years—her family sought out a suitable husband for her, and she was married in due course. This man, according to the Jewish custom, was to be a near relation of the maiden, if, as is generally held in the case of Our Lady, she was an heiress. It will then be well here to examine the relationship between Mary and Joseph.

According to the Jewish custom the genealogical tables, which were kept with great care, only give the descent through the father, and do not give the descent through the mother. Since our Lord was supposed to be the son of Joseph, His descent from David is given through His legal father. But as it was likewise the custom for husband and wife to be closely akin, the descent of the father contained that of the mother. The genealogy of Joseph is given both by St. Matthew and by St. Luke. In these lists, with the exception of two names which are common to both, the lists are completely different.

The whole question of the genealogy of Christ is full

[3] *Fouard*, I, Ch. vi.

of difficulties, and too vast a subject to be dealt with here. But from various tables which have been drawn up it may be shown that, by making certain hypotheses —reasonable, but not exempt from difficulties—there is no contradiction between St. Matthew and St. Luke. For example, Didon says:

"How are we to explain the genealogy of Luke, and its difference from that of Matthew? If, according to the former, Joseph has Jacob for father, how, according to the latter, is he 'of Heli'? The answer would appear to be simple.

"It is sufficient to ask who was Heli? Now, as can be established from several passages in Scripture, Heli is by abbreviation Heliakim, and Heliakim the synonym of Joachim. Joachim, according to the universal and constant tradition, was the father of Mary and the father-in-law of Joseph. By marrying the daughter of Heli, Joseph became the legal heir and son of Heli, so that St. Luke, by basing his genealogical table on the latter, has, in reality, given the paternal descent of Mary and Jesus. The vague expression *tou*, in Greek, 'who was of,' according to the translation of the Vulgate, used by St. Luke to describe the connection of these descendants from Joseph to Adam and to God Himself, is capable, because of its indeterminism, of three different meanings: it indicates a legal relationship of Joseph to Heli, a natural relationship between the others, a dependence of creature of Adam on God."—(Didon, II, Append.)[4]

[4] This view is supported by the following: "Holzmeister has recently advanced a very acceptable hypothesis in 'Ein Erklärungsversuch der

In this way the descent of Christ *ex semine David* through Mary is brought out. An examination of the table also shows that Joseph is not only the legal descendant of David but also a natural one. And although the genealogy of St. Luke indicates the natural descent of Mary and Jesus, it does so incidentally as being contained in the official genealogy of Joseph.

It is held by many that Mary lost her parents at an early age, and that before their deaths she was presented in the Temple. Others hold that during her early years she lived with her parents in Jerusalem, and received some special education and instruction in the Temple. From the fact that the Church celebrates a Feast of the Presentation on November 21st, we may deduce that there is a tradition to that effect. The Office read on that day contains a lesson from St. John Damascene, in which he states that Mary was born in Jerusalem, and placed in the Temple in order to grow up in the House of God and prepare herself for her great destiny away from the world. Those who hold this opinion give reasons for believing that there was some portion of the Temple in which children thus dedicated might live and be cared for. We are told that Anna "departed not

Lukasgenealogie' in the 'Zeitschrift fur Kath. Theol.' (1923, p. 184 *et seq.*): (1) The pedigree is to be regarded as being that of Joseph as stated in Luke. (2) Nevertheless the oldest tradition introduces the Mother of God. (3) Joseph entered the family of Mary as son-in-law to Heli (mentioned also in the Talmud as the father of Mary) by a kind of adoption, which is highly probable if Mary was an heiress, and it is in this sense that he is the 'son of Heli.' This adopted parentage did not, however, push the natural parentage into the background, as would a Levitical marriage, so that Joseph really possessed a double pedigree. The universal belief of earliest Christianity was that Mary was also of the race of David."—Reatz, *Life of Christ*, p. 27, footnote.

from the Temple, by fasting and prayer, serving day and night" (Luke ii, 37), but this may not necessarily mean that she actually lived in the Temple. Mary might very well have lived outside and received instruction in the Temple. We can only surmise as to the nature of the instruction received by Mary in her early years. It would certainly be that given to other Jewish maidens to fit her to take her place in the normal life of a Jewish woman, and up to the advent of Christianity it was the destiny of a Jewish maiden to be married.

It is generally held that it was during these early years that Mary, under the influence of some exceptional grace, dedicated herself to God either by a firm resolution or by vow. There is no Scriptural evidence that Mary had made a full vow, although that such was the case is generally held. It is suggested by St. Bonaventure and others that her desire was to become the handmaid of her who would be chosen to be the mother of the promised Messiah, whose advent was at the time eagerly expected. Such a resolution presented difficulties, for voluntary virginity was unheard of, although celibacy on the part of men was not uncommon. Many prophets and holy men were unmarried. The position of an unmarried maiden living in the world would have been intolerable.

CHAPTER II

THE BETROTHAL AND MARRIAGE OF MARY AND JOSEPH

"Joseph the husband of Mary, of whom was born Jesus, who is called Christ."—(Matt. i, 16)

MARRIAGE among the Jews proceeded by two stages; the bethrothal or espousals, and the reception of the bride into the home of her husband, signifying the consummation of the marriage. The betrothal was a family festival to which guests might be invited, chosen from relatives of the two families, who served as witnesses of the contract. The rite consisted of an interchange of promises, each saying to the other, "Behold thou art betrothed to me," or some such phrase. This engagement was sometimes put in writing. A certain sum of money, as a pledge of the bridegroom's fidelity, was handed to the bride and was retained by her. A certain sum payable to the father of the bride, and to be handed over to him at the time of the marriage, in compensation for the help and assistance she had rendered in her home, was also stipulated. This was called "the Mokar."

The entry of the bride into her new home and the consummation of the marriage did not usually take place until an interval—often as long as a year—had elapsed from the betrothal. A custom enjoined that during this

interval there was to be no personal intercourse whatever between the espoused couple. In practice the espousals had the force of a marriage—*ratum sed non con-
summatum*—and, if the espoused couple violated this
custom and a child were conceived, it was looked on as
legitimate. If the bride were unfaithful, she was liable to
the same penalties as a woman guilty of adultery. During the interval the contract might be broken by mutual
consent or for some special reason, such as unfaithful-
ness.[1]

[1] The agreement on the purchase-money constitutes the betrothal
of the young couple. Thenceforth they may not see or speak with each
other until after the wedding. Should an accidental meeting take place,
each is supposed to look the other way. This explains the action of
Rebecca when she saw for the first time her intended husband, Isaac,
in the distance; she at once descended from her camel and covered her
face with her veil. As the bride is veiled at the wedding, one can understand the possibility of such an accident as happened to Jacob when
the less attractive Leah was deceitfully substituted for the promised
Rachel (Gen. xxix, 23). This would be quite impossible in ordinary
cases, for the bridegroom's female relatives assist in arraying the bride
for the wedding. But Jacob, alone in a strange land, had no such safeguard against imposture."— Edmund Power, S.J., *Studies,* Vol. IX
(1920), p. 405.
It is reasonable to conclude from the fact that the same custom
existed long before the time of Christ which is now found in the Holy
Land that it also existed when Jesus was born.
Cf. also Lagrange in his Commentary on Matt. i, 18, who states that
any marital intercourse between the betrothed during the interval
would be looked on as "irregular." At the time of the marriage ceremony the bride was *de jure* a virgin.
"From the moment of betrothal both parties were regarded, and
treated in law (as to inheritance, adultery, need of formal divorce) as
if they had actually married, except as regards their living together."—
(*Edersheim,* I, p. 354.)
Cf. also Fouard, II. *The Visitation:* "When we recall how strict was
the seclusion which custom had imposed on a young Jewess after her
betrothal."
Cf. also Hastings' *Dictionary of the Gospels: Marriage.*

The festivities which characterised a Jewish wedding are described in many of the Lives of Christ, and are familiar to all in the story of the Wedding Feast of Cana. The account given in Fouard's *Life of Christ* ought to be read in connection with the marriage of Mary and Joseph. Both events probably took place in the same district, and from the Gospel account the social rank of both couples would seem to have been the same. There does not seem to have been any special religious rite involved in the marriage ceremony. The celebration consisted chiefly of a banquet, at which much wine was consumed, and is described as a gay, noisy and sometimes a not very sober event. The bride has been arrayed with as much magnificence as possible.

"The bridegroom and his companions enter within the dwelling of the young maiden, and, taking her by the hand, he leads her towards the threshold; and there he receives the tables of stone on which is inscribed the dowry; whereupon, in merry marching train, the guests retrace their way back to the house of the fortunate youth. A banquet is there made ready, which always lasted for many a long hour, enlivened by gay enigmas and sallies of wit. At the end of the banquet—which ends during the night—guests conduct the lady to the nuptial chamber where her couch was set in state beneath a canopy, sometimes (if we may credit Jewish authorities) under a bower of blossoms."—(Fouard, Vol. I, Ch. V.)

The above account is a synthesis compiled from many scriptural texts, and was, no doubt, subject to modifi-

cation, but it describes an event of great gaiety, and con-
gratulations to the happy pair on their marriage. After
the bride has been thus publicly received by her husband, the marriage was considered to have been consummated and indissoluble—except by divorce.

Especially in Galilee everything connected with betrothal and marriage "was planned with care, so as to
bear the impress of sanctity, and also to wear the aspect
of gladness." [2] It was taken for granted—except in the
case of a widow—that the bride was a virgin. "Outside
Judea the bride was a virgin *de jure*."—(Lagrange: *Com-
ment.*, Luke i, 27.) The marriage procession and all
connected with the bride's adornment were calculated to
emphasise this fact. Such was the marriage of Mary and
Joseph, which Fouard and Fillion describe in detail.

But there were other reasons why the marriage of
Mary and Joseph was to be perfect in every respect. It
was to be the model of Christian marriage, which is a
Sacrament. In his Apostolic Letter, *Neminem fugit*, read
in the Office of the Feast of the Holy Family, Pope Leo
XIII says: "When God in His mercy determined to accomplish the work of man's renewal, now through long
ages awaited, He so appointed and ordained this work,
that its very earliest beginnings might exhibit to the
world the august spectacle of a Family divinely constituted, in which all men might behold a perfect model
of domestic life and of all virtue and holiness." It was,
too, necessary that He who, as a child of a human

---

[2] Edersheim. The account given by this writer of the Jewish marriage
is well worth reading. He says: "It was regarded as a sacrament," and
"thus the bridal pair on the marriage day symbolised the union of
God with Israel."—(I, p. 352-355.)

mother, was to elevate marriage to be a Sacrament and restore matrimony to its original dignity, should Himself come into the world of a marriage perfect in all respects not only in the sight of God but also of men. And as the Messiah He was to be believed to be the descendant of David: "He could not be hailed as the Messiah unless He was believed to be the son of David. This He was through Joseph, whom everyone looked on as His father."—(Lagrange, p. 29.) The marriage of Mary and Joseph would in all things conform to the best traditions of the Jewish people among whom they lived. It was under the veil of human marriage that the mystery of the Incarnation was decreed by God to take place. Joseph was a "just man" in the fullest sense of the word, and Mary the ideal virgin adorned with all the virtues and beauty of soul which throughout the ages have inspired writers and artists in their greatest achievements. Yet in the eyes of their neighbours their marriage was like others, as Didon says: "This marriage had nothing, except the perfection of the two spouses, to distinguish it from others." (p. 47).

When, then, Mary approached the termination of her stay at the Temple, the question of her marriage arose automatically. A young woman would seem to have had very little to say as to the selection of her future husband, which was a matter to be arranged by her parents or relations, probably with the advice of the priests; but there is no reason to suppose that her inclinations were not consulted on the matter. This would have been especially expected in the case of a maiden who had lived near to or within the precincts of the Temple. Up to this time the life of Mary was secluded, and probably away from her family. It is generally held that at this time her parents were dead. But there is nothing to suggest that she had no intercourse with her relations. Indeed it is impossible not to believe that, on the occasions of their frequent visits to Jerusalem for the celebration of the various feasts, which every good Jew looked on as a sacred obligation, they did not often see and converse with their young kinswoman. Among these visitors Joseph would certainly be included—and here he first enters into the life of Mary.

That Joseph was a near relative of Mary is held by every authority. The Gospel does not tell us so directly, but the fact may be adduced from the whole plan of the Incarnation. Neither are we told in what degree they were related. St. Thomas uses the unusual word *propinquissimam*—"the very closest"—applied to Mary's relationship to Joseph. This too, is as we have seen, the conclusion arrived at from a close study of the genealogies given by Luke and Matthew (see p. 8). Joseph, then, as Mary's nearest of kin and head of the family— supposing her parents to have died—would have the right as well as the duty of knowing and interesting himself in all that concerned her well-being and progress. This is hardly a mere surmise; we may look on it as certain.

Joseph was a "just man." This means in the first place that he was a strict observer of the law and well versed in the Scriptures; and secondly, that he was a good and holy man, and, in the designs of God, possessed of all those qualities which his great mission demanded. We may, without any great call on the imagination, be sure that during these years these two chosen souls learned to realise the holiness of each other, and that Mary would have confided her secret to him—to whom she looked up and in whom she trusted as one probably somewhat older than herself, and as her natural guardian and protector. And in this way Mary and Joseph would have been drawn to each other with a pure and holy affection. May we not conclude that Mary confided to him the inspiration she had received to dedicate her virginity to God? Nor may we consider that such a confidence would be any reflection on the purity and delicacy of her soul. Versed as she was in the Scriptures—as the Annunciation itself proves—it is impossible that she would have been unaware of what we sometimes refer to as "the facts of life," as indeed is evident from her query to the Angel Gabriel. To her wise and straightforward character —which appears throughout the whole Gospel story— there would be no occasion for false modesty in her dealings with an intimate and beloved relation such as Joseph.

According to the designs of God, as afterwards appears from the Gospels, it was necessary that Mary should be married. It seems certain that at this time she had no idea that she was to be the Virgin-Mother of the Messiah. But God was bringing about all things sweetly. Theologians give many reasons why Mary should be married. For us it is enough to look at the matter from the point of view of her contemporaries. In the first place, the position of any unmarried maiden would have been anomalous and difficult: that of an unmarried mother would, humanly speaking, have been intolerable and degrading both for mother and child. The claim that she was the Virgin-Mother of the promised Messiah would have earned for her the reputation of being a visionary. The fact is that at this time the famous prophecy of Isaias: "Behold a virgin shall conceive and bear a son: and his name shall be called Emmanuel" (vii, 14) does not seem to have been understood. No one of the Jewish women who, we are told, hoped that she might be privileged to be the mother of the Messiah, determined to remain a virgin. As we shall consider later, Mary, who in her humility aspired to no such honour, did make such a resolve under the influence of an altogether special inspiration.

The good name of Mary and the honour of the Son she was destined to bring forth demanded, according to the decrees of God, that He should be known among men as the son of a father and mother united in lawful wedlock. Therefore it was part of God's plan that Mary should have a husband. And God provided a husband who would fulfil perpectly all the requisite conditions. In the first place, according to the perfect observance of the law: "Let them (heiresses) marry whom they will, only so that it be men of their own tribe, lest the possession of the children of Israel be mingled from tribe to tribe. For all men shall marry wives of their own tribe and kindred. And all women shall take husbands of the same tribe; that the inheritance may remain in the families" (Numbers xxxvi, 7-8). Among the Jews the genealogies, so carefully preserved, took no account of women. Descent was derived through the husband.

Since the promised Messiah was to be a descendant

of David, it was therefore necessary that Jesus should be known publicly as the Son of David. But it was equally necessary that He should actually have the blood of David in His veins—ex semine David.[3] In the case of Jesus this could only be through His mother Mary. It was therefore necessary that she should herself be of the family of David. It is clear that these two ends would be achieved by her marriage to a very near relation. Christ's actual descent through the Virgin Mary would be identical with His legal descent through Joseph. Hence Mary's husband, both on account of the observance of the law, and in order to carry out the designs of God, was to be looked for among her own kindred. Evidently such a husband must be a man possessing altogether exceptional qualities of nature and grace.

In the choice of Mary's husband, the priests and members of the family who would make the choice would only consider the matter from the ordinary human point of view. They knew nothing of Mary's resolution to preserve her virginity, or of her destiny. The husband they would approve of must possess the ordinary human qualities required in one who was to be the husband of a maiden known to be so holy and, there can be no doubt, so much beloved and venerated by all who knew her. Theologians discuss at length the qualities of such a man, but have to base their opinions on what would be considered fitting and becoming in the eyes of men. For, as we have pointed out, Joseph and Mary were to appear to the world as man and wife in the usual acceptance of

---

[3] ". . . concerning His Son, who was made to Him of the seed of David, according to the flesh . . ." (Rom. i, 3).

the words. There should be no great disparity in their ages, and hence they conclude that the chosen husband was in the prime of life, and fitted to support his wife and her Child by his work. He should have the qualities of head and heart which would ensure for her the sympathy and strength of character on which she could rely in the ordinary conditions of married life. He should have for his young wife love and affection, and be one to whom she too would look up in reverence and love. Above all, he should be possessed of holiness and love of God in order to be the worthy husband of one whose sancitity was known to them all.

Now, of all her relations, there was none more suitable than Joseph. Of all the qualities enumerated, the Gospel tells us directly only of two; but they are the most essential and, to the thinking mind, include the others. Joseph was the "son of David," and he was a "just man." And, as we have seen, it can be gathered from the genealogies that he was of the same tribe and family as Mary. Hence, it is not surprising that Joseph was approved of by all as a fitting husband for the virgin Mary. If this judgment was a sound one for natural reasons, it was still more so in the designs of God. We have observed that it is natural to believe that she had confided to him the great secret of her dedication of herself to God; that she would at least have done so before marriage with anyone is certain. Many of the Fathers and theologians are of opinion that, independently of Mary, Joseph too had resolved to abstain from the use of marriage. Whether this is true or not, it is clear from the Gospel story that he fell in completely with the views and resolve of Mary. As illustrating the views held by the saints and fathers, we may cite the following passage from a sermon on St. Joseph by St. Bernardine of Siena, which is read among the Offices of the Feast of his Patronage:

"It is a general rule of all special favours conferred upon any rational creature that whenever divine grace chooses anyone for some particular grace, or for some high station, it likewise bestows on the person so chosen all the gifts necessary for that high station and furnishes them abundantly. This was verified in a marked degree in St. Joseph, the supposed father of our Lord Jesus Christ, and the true spouse of the Queen of the World and the Mistress of the Angels; who was chosen by the eternal Father as the faithful guide and guardian of His chiefest treasures, that is to say, of His own Son, and of Joseph's Spouse, which duty he most faithfully discharged. Wherefore the Lord says: Good and faithful servant, enter thou into the joy of the Lord . . . Since the marriage of Mary and Joseph was a real marriage contracted by divine inspiration, and since marriage is so close a union of souls that the bridegroom and the bride are said to be one person, which may be called, as it were, the perfection of unity; how can any discerning person think that the Holy Ghost would unite in such a union, the soul of such a virgin to any soul that did not resemble hers in the works of virtue? Therefore I believe that this man, St. Joseph, was adorned with the most pure virginity, the most profound humility, the most ardent

love and charity towards God, the loftiest contemplation. And since the Virgin knew that he was given her
by the Holy Ghost to be her spouse, and the faithful
guardian of her virginity, and to share besides in affectionate love and indulgent care towards the most divine Offspring of God; therefore I believe that she
loved St. Joseph sincerely with all the affection of her
heart." [4]

From these considerations it is clear that in becoming
espoused to Joseph, Mary knew that her resolution of
perpetual virginity would, according to the will of God,
be assured. In all else she would be the loving and beloved wife of this good and unselfish man. In order to
carry out what they both believed to be the will of God,
Mary sacrificed the dearest wish of every Jewish woman
—to be a mother. Theirs was to be a virgin-marriage in
fact, although in the sight of men they would be in all
things man and wife as all other married people. In the
history of the Church there are many examples of married people who, after years of married life in the full
meaning of the word, agreed to live as brother and
sister. But there is perhaps a difficulty as to how it is
possible for two people to undertake all the mutual
obligations promised at the time of marriage, and at the
same time to resolve on and even to be vowed to virginity. But there is no contradiction involved. Marriage
confers the possession of certain mutual rights and duties
on husband and wife, but does not impose the obligation

---

[4] The English Version of the Roman Breviary: Spring Part (London,
1936) contains many homilies by the Fathers of the Church on St.
Joseph.

of exercising these rights. There is no real marriage unless these rights are accepted at least implicitly along
with the obligations that accompany them.[5] The primary
object of marriage is the generation of children through
marital intercourse, and their support and education;
but there are other secondary objects which may constitute the marriage bond, such as those which arise from
mutual affection and companionship, and all that this
implies.

While assuming all the rights and obligations required in order to receive the sacrament and complete
the contract of marriage, it is at the same time permis-
sible for those contracting marriage to agree mutually—
even under vow—not to exercise the right they possess
of using the natural means of generating children—in
other words, to live in a state of virginity. The difference between having a right and exercising it may perhaps be best illustrated by considering the simple vows
of poverty made by the members of religious orders. According to the constitutions of these bodies the members
continue to retain, after their vows, the dominion or
ownership of any property they may have possessed up
to the taking of these vows. But by their vows they bind
themselves by a serious obligation not to make use of

[5] The essence of the marriage contract is that each of the parties
should possess the right to marital intercourse with the other. Even in a
virgin-marriage this right must exist even though it be not exercised. A
difficulty would arise from the supposition that either or both parties
made the non-exercise of this right an *absolute* condition at the time
of their marriage. Suarez states that it is *de fide* that there was a true
marriage in the strict sense of the word between Mary and Joseph. He
is therefore logically bound to hold that there was a certain conditional
element in Mary's vow or resolution to preserve her virginity, such, for
example, as "unless God wishes otherwise."

any such property without the permission of their legitimate superiors. For all practical purposes their position in the religious life is the same as that of those who never possessed money or the right to use it. If a religious who possessed the right to own property were, without permission, to make use of this right, he or she would sin grievously against the vow of poverty, but the sin would not be one of theft or dishonesty. In the same way, if married people who had bound themselves by a vow of virginity were to violate their vow and exercise their marital rights without dispensation from their vow they would sin, but the sin would be against the vow and not against the sacrament of marriage.

Such was the marriage of Mary and Joseph. They were truly married, and undertook, implicitly at least, all the obligations of married life while agreeing to live together as brother and sister. The very existence of this agreement constituted a further bond of mutual love and confidence between them.

CHAPTER III

THE ANNUNCIATION

"Behold a virgin shall conceive and bring forth a Son."
—(Is. vii, 14).

"And in the sixth month, the angel Gabriel was sent from God into a city of Galilee, called Nazareth, to a virgin espoused to a man whose name was Joseph, of the house of David: and the virgin's name was Mary. And the angel being come in, said unto her: Hail, full of grace, the Lord is with thee: blessed art thou among women. Who, having heard, was troubled at his saying and thought within herself what manner of salutation this should be. And the angel said to her: Fear not, Mary, for thou hast found grace with God. Behold thou shalt conceive in thy womb and bring forth a son: and thou shalt call his name Jesus. He shall be great and shall be called the Son of the Most High. And the Lord God shall give unto him the throne of David his father: and he shall reign in the house of Jacob for ever. And of his kingdom there shall be no end. And Mary said to the angel: How shall this be done, because I know not man? And the angel answering, said to her: The Holy Ghost shall come upon thee and the power of the Most High shall overshadow thee. And therefore also the Holy that shall be born of thee shall be called the Son of God. And behold thy cousin Elizabeth, she also hath conceived a son in her old age: and this is the sixth month with her that is called barren. Because no word shall be impossible with God. And Mary said:

Behold the handmaid of the Lord: be it done to me according to thy word. And the angel departed from her."—St. Luke i, 26-38.

THE above passage from St. Luke and that from St. Matthew quoted in Chapter V give us the account of the coming of Jesus Christ into the world in His human nature. While they clearly tell of the miraculous conception, the virgin birth and perpetual virginity of Our Lady, they present many difficulties, the solution of which demands an examination of the original Greek and Latin texts, and of the writings of the Fathers and other such documents, which would be impossible in a short account such as this. And, even when all available information has been obtained, there still remains uncertainty about many matters of detail. One of these problems is whether the final marriage ceremony of the marriage of Mary and Joseph took place before or after the Annunciation.

While all are agreed that the betrothal had already taken place, there is a difference of opinion as to the time of the marriage. The majority of modern writers on the life of Christ, and commentators such at Patrizi, Knabenbauer and Lagrange, are of opinion that the marriage of Mary and Joseph took place when Our Lady returned from her visit to Elizabeth. St. Thomas, Suarez and Bossuet, with commentators such as Á Lapide, Maldonatus and Bucceroni, consider it probable that the marriage had already been celebrated before the Annunciation. Fathers of the Church and other authorities are cited for both opinions. Those who hold that Mary and Joseph were married and living in the same house before the Annunciation are of opinion that otherwise their contemporaries would have reason to suspect that Jesus was not—as He was *de facto* thought by all to be—the son of Joseph (cf. Ch. II). For us who know the whole story it is not a matter of very great importance. It is clear that in every respect their marrige would have been in conformity with the customs and traditions then prevailing in Galilee. Thus in the eyes of their Jewish contemporaries, who knew nothing of the inner history of the Incarnation, all occurred so that Jesus appeared among men as the son of Joseph and Mary through human generation. So well was the secret of His miraculous origin kept, it is certain that there was never any question of Joseph not being the earthly father of Christ in the ordinary meaning of the word. St. Luke tells us that when "Jesus himself was beginning about the age of thirty" He was "supposed" (that is to say, "believed by all") to be the "Son of Joseph." The present state of our knowledge has been summed up by P. Lebreton, one of the foremost of modern Biblical scholars, as follows:

"Thus the two Gospels that record our Lord's infancy appear from the purely historical standpoint to be derived from most authentic sources: S. Luke inspired by our Lady's own recollections, and S. Matthew based on a tradition originating with S. Joseph himself. These two traditions, authoritative in the highest degree, are none the less independent and fragmentary: *the order of events may be sometimes uncertain* [1] and, above all, the narrative as a whole

---

[1] Italics ours.

remains incomplete. But at least these fragments have a historical value of the first order and at the same time a freshness and liveliness of expression that make them one of the most precious religious treasures that we possess." *La Vie et l'Enseignement de Jésus Christ Notre Seigneur*, par Jules Lebreton, S.J. (7 Ed. Paris, 1935, p. 45.) See also P. Durant, S.J.: *L'Enfance de Jésus Christ*, p. xv, note.

It is definitely implied that the Annunciation took place in Our Lady's abode. The Greek word used in the account of the visit of the Angel is correctly translated in the English version by the expression, "And the Angel being come in." Christian art has always represented the interview between Our Lady and the Angel as having taken place in her chamber when she was at prayer.

A similar angelic message had been sent to Zachary, announcing the conception of John the Baptist by his wife Elizabeth. He too was troubled, and asked: "Whereby shall I know this? for I am an old man; and my wife is advanced in years." And the Angel answering, said to him: "I am Gabriel who stand before God; and am sent to speak to thee, and to bring thee these good tidings. And behold thou shalt be dumb, and shalt not be able to speak until the day wherein these things shall come to pass; because thou hast not believed my words, which shall be fulfilled in their time" (Luke i, 11-20). The very coming of the angel was a sufficient sign. Mary did not doubt the angel's word nor ask for a sign, nor did she put the question merely from curiosity. She put the question because she had to. It was the

determination of Mary, as we have seen, to be united to
her husband Joseph by the ties of a true marriage, but
by a virgin-marriage. They had agreed that this marriage
was always to remain such, unless God clearly intimated
that they should enter into the relations of ordinary marriage. It was with the object of being informed as to the
will of God that Mary asked how she was to become the
mother of a son.

This explanation implies that, at the time of the Annunciation, Mary did not look on the prophecy of Isaias,
"Behold a virgin shall conceive and bear a son" (vii,
14), as applying to herself. Indeed it seems certain that
in her day the prophecy was not looked on in the sense
afterwards explained by St. Matthew (i, 18-23), and in
which Mary herself was unconsciously taking her part.
It is clear that she did not look on herself as the Virgin,
for otherwise there would be no reason to ask the question. That the text of Isaias was not interpreted in this
sense is the opinion of modern scholars. Edersheim, who
thoroughly examined the Messianic texts, recognised as
such by Jewish writers, gives a list of about a hundred
taken from Isaias alone, but makes no mention of vii,
14 (Vol. ii, pp. 273, et seq.) Edersheim, who holds
firmly the fact of the virgin-birth of Christ, says in his
account of the Annunciation: "And the words which
she spake, were not of trembling doubt, that required
to lean on the staff of a 'sign,' but rather those of inquiry,
for the further guidance of a willing self-surrender"
(Vol i, p. 151).

Commenting on the word virgin, Dr. Kissane says:

". . . The prophet chose a word which is so elastic in meaning that it can refer to a virgin and yet not exclude the notion of child-bearing. As noted above, the circumstances of Emmanuel's birth do not form an essential part of the 'sign,' the prophet was probably not aware of the full import of the revelation of which he was the medium. The word he chose is somewhat vague, and further revelation was needed to unfold its meaning. The use of the word *parthenos* in the Septuagint probably indicates that this further revelation had come before that Version was formed; the fulfilment of the revelation in the person of Christ has proved that in fact the word referred to a virgin in the strict sense" (*The Book of Isaiah*, vol. I, p. 89).

It is sometimes said by pious writers (e. g., St Anselm) that Our Lady was prepared to forego the dignity of becoming the mother of the Messiah rather than sacrifice her virginity. One thing is certain, that, before all, she was the "handmaid of the Lord," and that she had no other will than to do the will of her heavenly Father. This is clearly shown in the *Magnificat*, as will be pointed out later. We have seen that, consistently with being truly married—her resolution or vow—there must have been some such condition attached to it as "if it be God's will" (see p. 23). Her question to the Angel can then be understood as not only a reasonable question, but as one which—in her ignorance, or at least uncertainty, of the virgin birth—had to be put. This is the view of St. Bernard and St. Albert the Great, among others. The words of St. Bernard are:

"But Mary said to the Angel: how shall this be done, because I know not man? At first she kept a prudent silence, but she was in doubt what this salutation might be, and she preferred in humility to give no answer rather than risk speaking of what she did not understand. Now, however, she was strengthened and prepared; for while the angel spoke externally God disposed her heart, for the Lord was present with her when the angel said, 'The Lord is with thee.'

"Thus animated to keep out fear by the spirit of faith, she said to the Angel: 'How shall this be done, for I know not man?' She doubts not the fact, but only inquires about the manner of its accomplishment. She says not 'Will it be done?' but 'How will it be done?' As if she would say: Since my Lord knows, and my conscience bears me witness, that His handmaid has made a vow to know no man, by what law shall it please Him to work this wonder? If I must be dispensed from my vow that I may bring forth such a son, I rejoice on account of the son, but I grieve because of my vow. Nevertheless His will be done. If, however, as a virgin I may bring forth this Son—and it is not impossible if He so will it—then I shall know that He hath regard to the humility of His handmaid. How, then, shall this be done, for I know not man?" [2]

A Lapide, commenting on these words, cites a very similar passage from the writings of St. Albert the Great. When we examine the passage at the head of this

[2] St. Bernard, *Missus est.* Homily IV. Translated at St. Mary's Convent, York. London, 1909.

chapter we notice that the account of the Annunciation proceeds in several stages. The Angel comes in—presumably into the chamber where Mary was praying—and addresses her in words which must have seemed strange to a simple maiden; she is troubled at these words, and thinks what it might mean—the use of the imperfect tense implies that she dwelt on them while the Angel spoke; she is reassured in the same words as those already addressed to Zachary, and which were to be said to Joseph, "Fear not"; at once the announcement of the "great things" for which she was destined was made to her; then it was that Mary asked how was she, a virgin who was resolved to remain one, to become a mother; then it was that the wonderful mystery of the Incarnation was revealed to her; and Mary said her *fiat*. And the Angel departed from her.

The whole event only occupied a few moments. Mary was not kept in suspense. There is in fact a great resemblance in the accounts of the three "annunciations" to Zachary, Mary and later to Joseph. In each there is a prompt delivery of the message just at the moment when those who received it might be expected to "be troubled."

The angelic message included a sign—unasked by Mary—by which she should be reassured that the conception of a son by her, a virgin, was the will of God, with whom no word shall be impossible: "And behold thy cousin Elizabeth, she also hath conceived a son in her old age: and this is the sixth month with her that is called barren."

But it would seem that the extraordinary fact of the

conception by Elizabeth must also have been generally known in Nazareth by this time. Elizabeth had "hid herself five months," and the Annunciation was "in the sixth month," so that there was ample time for the news, which had evidently become known in "Juda" at the end of the five months, to reach Nazareth before Mary went on her visit. A young woman would evidently need some ostensible motive for leaving her home on such a journey. Providence had arranged for that. St. Luke tells us that, "Mary rising up in those days, went into the hill country with haste into a city of Juda." The words "in those days" indicate that Mary did not set out immediately after the Angel's visit, but that she did so within a few days, and that she lost no time on the way; she would have had to make some preparations. Lagrange suggests that she joined a caravan going to Jerusalem, perhaps for the Passover. This suggestion is also of interest as supporting the view that Christ was born during the winter, which would be nine months later than the Passover, and took place about the same time of year as our Easter. Mary would then have arrived at Jerusalem, and possibly celebrated the great feast along with her companions. St. Luke does not tell us the name of the "city of Juda" where Zachary lived.

Such is the historical account of the greatest event which has ever happened since the creation, the coming of the uncreated Son of God into the world in human form. Both St. Matthew and St. Luke give some idea of the greatness of the Child who was to be born. St. Luke tells us that:

"He shall be great and shall be called the son of
the most high. And the Lord God will give unto him
the throne of David his father: and he shall reign in
the house of Jacob for ever. And of his kingdom there
shall be no end."

And St. Matthew tells us that:

"All this was done that it might be fulfilled which
the Lord spoke by the prophet, saying:

"*Behold a virgin shall be with child, and bring forth
a son, and they shall call his name Emmanuel, which
being interpreted is, God with us.*"

But it is St. John who reveals to us the full and awful
significance of the mystery of the Incarnation of the
"only-begotten of the Father," the "Word made flesh."
While Matthew and Luke give us the human genealogies of Christ the Son of David, John passes from earth
to heaven and gives the divine genealogy, as it were, of
Christ the Son of God:

In the beginning was the Word, and the Word was
with God, and the Word was God.
The same was in the beginning with God.
All things were made by him: and without him was
made nothing that was made.
In him was life, and the life was the light of men:
And the light shineth in darkness, and the darkness
did not comprehend it. . . .
That was the true light, which enlighteneth every
man that cometh into this world.

He was in the world, and the world was made by him, and the world knew him not.

He came into his own, and his own knew him not.

But as many as received him, he gave them power to be made the sons of God, to them that believe in his name.

Who are born, not of blood, nor of the will of the flesh, nor of the will of man, but of God.

And the Word was made flesh, and dwelt among us (and we saw his glory, the glory as it were of the only-begotten of the Father) full of grace and truth.

In a single flight John traces the coming of Jesus Christ, true God and true man, from the bosom of the Father to the womb of the Virgin Mary. It was through her that the Word was made Flesh. As sin and death came into the world through the disobedience of a woman, so forgiveness and life were to come in the Person of Jesus Christ, in the words of St. Paul, "made of a woman" (Gal. iv, 4), and the Virgin Mary was that woman. The Church keeps this great fact in our memories by reading the Gospel of St. John in the Mass, in the *Angelus* which all good Catholics say thrice daily, and in the Creed read at Mass:

"I believe in one God, the Father Almighty, maker of heaven and earth, and of all things visible and invisible. And in one Lord Jesus Christ, the only-begotten Son of God, born of the Father before all ages. God of God; Light of Light; true God of true God; begotten not made; consubstantial with the Father, by whom all things were made. Who for us men, and for our salvation, came down from heaven, and was incarnate by the Holy Ghost of the Virgin Mary; and was made man."

This is the foundation of the veneration in which Mary is held throughout the Catholic Church and by every true Christian who believes in the Divinity of Christ, and it is on this account that the Catholic Church teaches that:

MARY IS THE MOTHER OF GOD

CHAPTER IV

THE VISITATION

"And Mary said: my soul doth magnify the Lord: and my spirit hath rejoiced in God my Saviour" (Luke i, 47, 48).

"And Mary rising up in those days, went into the hill country with haste into a city of Juda. And she entered into the house of Zachary, and saluted Elizabeth. And it came to pass that when Elizabeth heard the salutation of Mary, the infant leaped in her womb. And Elizabeth was filled with the Holy Ghost: and she cried out with a loud voice, and said: Blessed art thou among women, and blessed is the fruit of thy womb. And whence is this to me, that the mother of my Lord should come to me? For behold as soon as the voice of thy salutation sounded in my ears, the infant in my womb leaped for joy. And blessed art thou that hast believed, because those things shall be accomplished that were spoken to thee by the Lord. And Mary said: My soul doth magnify the Lord: and my spirit hath rejoiced in God my Saviour. Because he hath regarded the humility of his handmaid: for behold from henceforth all generations shall call me blessed. Because he that is mighty hath done great things to me: and holy is his name. And his mercy is from generation unto generations, to them that fear him. He hath shewed might in his arm: he hath scattered the proud in the conceit of their heart. He hath put down the mighty from their seat, and hath exalted the humble. He hath filled the hungry with good things: and the rich he hath sent empty away. He hath received Israel his servant, being mindful of his mercy. As he spoke to our fathers, to Abraham and to his seed for ever. And Mary abode with her about three months: and she returned to her own house."—(St. Luke i, 39-50.)

ST. LUKE does not tell us the name of the place where Zachary and Elizabeth resided, but according to a tradition which goes back to the fifth century, and which is adopted by modern writers, the "city of Juda" is Ain Karim, about five miles to the west of Jerusalem, which Mary could have reached alone without difficulty.[1]

Mary looked on the words of Gabriel as an invitation to her to visit her cousin Elizabeth, most probably in order to be with her as the birth of her child drew near. Living so near Jerusalem, it is reasonable to conclude that Elizabeth would have often visited Mary during the years she spent in or near the Temple, and that they were, therefore, united by ties of warm affection. Mary's first thought would have been to perform this act of charity and friendship. No doubt, too, she was glad to have an opportunity of confiding in this elderly kinswoman who, herself the recipient of a great favour, would rejoice with Mary on the great thing which He that is mighty had done to her. Mary's heart was full of joy, which she wished to share with another. The Church describes the virgin-mother as *gaudia matris habens cum virginitatis honore*—"having the joys of a mother with the honour of virginity."

The words of welcome uttered by Elizabeth assured her that God had also made known to Elizabeth that

[1] According to other authorities Zachary lived at Juttah, near Hebron, about thirty miles south of Jerusalem.

Mary was to bring forth the Messiah. And then it was
that Mary poured out from the fulness of her heart the
most beautiful of all the Canticles, her *Magnificat.* One
has but to read it to see how deeply it is influenced by
the literature of the Bible, but the matter is "in the
language of her own heart."

And Mary said:

"My soul doth magnify the Lord:
And my spirit hath rejoiced in God my Saviour.
Because he hath regarded the humility of his hand-
     maid:
For behold from henceforth all generations shall call
     me blessed.

Because he that is mighty hath done great things to
     me;
And holy is his name.
And his mercy is from generation to generation.
To them that fear him.

He hath showed might in his arm:
He hath scattered the proud in the conceit of their
     heart.
He hath put down the mighty from their seat,
And hath exalted the humble.
He hath filled the hungry with good things;
And the rich he hath sent empty away.

He hath received Israel, his servant,
Being mindful of his mercy:

As he spoke to our fathers,
To Abraham and to his seed for ever."

This exquisite hymn is not only the outpouring of a heart full of love and gratitude to her Father in heaven for His goodness to herself, and for His past and future benefits to her people. It gives the key to the whole character of Mary and her attitude towards her God. Mary was daughter of the Father, and spouse of the Holy Ghost before she became mother of the Son.

Mary had "found grace with God," and He had "done great things" to her. He had chosen her to be the mother of His Divine Son. She had believed, and had accepted with joy the wonderful destiny and blessing of becoming the Mother of God. We do not know in what terms Mary saluted Elizabeth, but when they were uttered the child leaped in her womb, and Elizabeth, filled with the Holy Ghost, cried out in a loud voice and said: "Blessed art thou among women, and blessed is the fruit of thy womb"—words which are repeated throughout the world millions of times each day. And Elizabeth goes on to tell Mary why she is blessed, "And blessed art thou that hast believed, because these things shall be accomplished that were spoken to thee by the Lord." This is the blessedness from which all her other blessings spring. But she would not have attained that unique blessedness if she had not been by God's grace and her own co-operation the humble and immaculate "hand-maid of the Lord." Later on, her Son showed His esteem of her conformity to the will of God when He told those who praised her who bore Him that His mother was blessed because she heard the will of God and kept it. Mere blood-relationship, even with Him, would not make her blessed—if *per impossibile* she herself had not been holy.

It is not part of our object to dwell on the poetic or literary qualities of this Canticle, which has been the subject of unqualified admiration by all. It reflects the highest traditions of Hebrew poetry and many of the expressions used by Mary and other women of the Bible, especially of Judith and Anna the mother of Samuel. During her stay in the Temple or at home Mary would have learned and committed to memory these outpourings of hearts under the influence of deep emotions. The canticle of Anna in particular would, no doubt, have influenced her profoundly. Samuel had in his youth served in the house of the Lord, and was especially favoured by God. The names of Anna and Heli which appear in that history would have reminded her of her own parents. The *Magnificat* was her own, and in it Mary expressed her own feelings, but the mode of doing so was strongly influenced by her own training and the history of her people.

From a consideration of the whole tenor of this hymn we may gather the feelings which filled Mary's heart, and form an estimate of her character. The following extracts indicate that the *Magnificat* came from a heart free from any impending sorrow:

Fillon says:

"Mary in turn, filled with the Spirit of God, which transforms her into a great poet, answers Elizabeth's

praise by chanting the *Magnificat*, a canticle sublime
in its simplicity. It was the overflowing of her heart,
which poured itself forth melodiously at the first occasion that offered. It is a lyric poem of serene and
majestic beauty. It transports us to an atmosphere of
peace and light, of calm joy and heavenly piety, in
which Mary's soul was living since she had become the
mother of the Word. Its serenity is in sharp contrast
to Elizabeth's ardent words. It is a sort of meditation
that Mary here makes, giving free rein to the feelings
and impressions that had arisen in her soul. Other
women of Israel had from time to time celebrated
marvellous events in beautiful canticles. Following
Miriam (the sister of Moses), Debora, Anne (the
mother of Samuel) and Judith, the Blessed Virgin
pays homage to her God in the same form. Her hymn,
in which we find all the characteristics of Hebrew
poetry, and which St. Augustine judges worthy of
being sung by *tympanistria nostra*, shows a lofty
nature, a fine intellect, profound religious feeling, and
a very just appreciation of the Jewish history to which
it refers" (i, p. 269).

Didon says:

"This inspired canticle passes out beyond all earthly
horizons, and closes the cycle of former times; it is
no longer hope calling for God, it is triumphant with
faith which sees and possesses Him; it is the hymn of
the new age, and the most splendid cry of gladness
which has ever come from a human heart" (p. 41).

Prat says:

"In it Mary gives full rein to the three sentiments which filled her soul; humble gratitude at the recollection of the great things which God had worked within her; admiration for the wisdom and mercy of Him who puts down the mighty and exalts the weak; finally, the joyous assurance that God is about to fulfil His promises by sending to His people a Liberator" (Vie de Jésus i, p. 67).

One who was not a Catholic wrote:

"But in St. Luke the picture is clothed with flesh and blood; the dream grows real. There is breath and poetry upon her lips. Her heart beats quicker at the angel's salutation . . . The Magnificat, chanted in so many churches, is the highest specimen of the subtle influence of the song of purity . . . It is a woman teaching in the Church for ever without usurpation of authority, but with a saintly quietness (I Tim. ii, 12), that knows no end. The psychologist seems to sound the depths of that nature—ever watching and keeping close the several single things which are so many special utterances of God; ever comparing them with and interpreting them by facts. He lets us see that as she has kept them closely, so she kept them on through all circumstances" (Dr. Alexander, The Leading Ideas of the Gospels, p. 113).

Having passed about three months with Elizabeth, Mary set out on her journey back to Nazareth. Whether she remained with her kinswoman until after the birth of

John is uncertain. If we were to form an opinion based on what ordinary feelings of kindness and sympathy would suggest, we should conclude that Mary remained until after the birth of the child to whom her own Child brought so great a blessing. However, the Gospel narrative leaves the matter doubtful.

A close examination of the circumstances of the miraculous conception and birth of Christ, who was "supposed to be the son of Joseph," and of the details given by St. Luke, indicates that the whole period of Mary's absence from Nazareth was almost exactly three months, neither many days more nor less. It seems probable that Mary departed from the home of Elizabeth either before the birth of John or very soon after it.

CHAPTER V

THE PERPLEXITY OF JOSEPH

"Joseph, son of David, fear not to take unto thee Mary thy wife" (Matt. i, 20).

"Now the generation of Christ was in this wise. When as His mother Mary was espoused to Joseph, before they came together, she was found with child, of the Holy Ghost. Whereupon Joseph her husband, being a just man, and not willing publicly to expose her, was minded to put her away privately. But while he thought on these things, behold the angel of the Lord appeared to him in his sleep, saying: 'Joseph, son of David, fear not to take unto thee Mary thy wife, for that which is conceived in her, is of the Holy Ghost. And she shall bring forth a son: and thou shalt call His name Jesus; for He shall save His people from their sins.' Now all this was done that it might be fulfilled which the Lord spoke by the prophet, saying: *Behold a virgin shall be with child, and bring forth a son, and they shall call His name Emmanuel*, which being interpreted is, *God with us*. And Joseph rising up from sleep, did as the angel of the Lord had commanded him, and took unto him his wife. And he knew her not till she brought forth her first-born son: and he called His name Jesus."—Matt. i, 18-25.

I⟊ is generally accepted as a fact that the two first chapters of St. Luke's Gospel—Our Lady's Gospel—are derived from her own account of what she narrates. Both the matter and the style are declared by critics to be distinctly Jewish and to contrast sharply with the rest of that Gospel. It is believed by many that Mary herself told her story direct to St. Luke; others are of opinion that he had it from a third person; for example, from the Beloved Disciple, who "took her to his own." In any case it is her Gospel. St. Matthew, on the other hand, writes from the point of view of Joseph. The question arises as to how the facts he narrates, dealing often with the inmost thoughts of Joseph, were conveyed to the Evangelist. It is most improbable that Joseph himself told Matthew these facts directly. It is however extremely probable that Joseph confided his part in the coming of Jesus to some relative as a precious record. When we look for the most likely person to have received this trust, the name of his brother, Cleophas—or Alpheus—at once suggests itself. His wife, Mary, was clearly on the most intimate terms with Our Lady, indicating that the two families were closely attached. When St. Matthew began collecting the matter of his Gospel, nothing is more likely than that he applied to Cleophas for his recollections. It has even been suggested that St. Matthew, who is described by St. Mark (ii, 14) as "the son of Alpheus," was his son, and the brother of St. James (*Dict. of the Bible*, Hastings). There is no proof of such a relationship. Again it is possible that Our Lord Himself may have included these facts in His discourse to the two disciples going to Emmaus, when "beginning at Moses and all the prophets, he expounded to them in all the scriptures the things that were concerning him" (Luke xxiv, 27). St. Matthew, as we know, was very prone to note the fulfilment of prophecies, as for example in the above passage. It is a curious fact that, as St. Luke notes, the name of one of these disciples was Cleophas! In any case it is clear that St. Matthew had sources at hand to supply the facts.[1]

The passage at the beginning of this chapter gives rise to many problems, and forms the subject of a great deal of discussion among Catholics themselves and other writers; but it affords much valuable information, and adds fresh proof of the divine origin and virgin-birth of our Saviour. To discuss the passage fully here would be quite impossible, and we must content ourselves with examining some of the more important points in the light of Scripture and the conclusions of the commentators.

It is clear from the passage just quoted that Joseph was not aware of the visit of the Angel Gabriel to Mary, and the miraculous conception of her Son. We have already dealt with the reasons which suggest themselves for this apparent want of confidence on the part of Mary. When, then, she "was found to be with child,"

[1] "St. Luke tells the tale from the standpoint of Mary herself, the mother watching and pondering lovingly over her own Child, marking His outward growth and progressive dedication to His Heavenly Father; full of charitable interest in Elizabeth also, and of the child who was to be the forerunner of her own. But, if in Luke we have the gospel of Mary, in Matthew we have the gospel of Joseph, bearing no less certain tokens of its origin. St. Matthew is not likely to have known Joseph; but several of the other Apostles would have known him, from whom he might learn the tale. It is the personal record of the master of the family, and of the anxieties which pressed upon him . . ."— (Introduction to Gospel of St. Matthew, *Westminster Version*, p. xxxvi.)

the perplexity of Joseph could only be accounted for by the fact that, on the one hand, he knew that he was not the father of her Child, and, on the other, that he did not associate the prophecy of Isaias with his virgin-spouse. As we have pointed out,[2] this fact indicates that the full meaning of the prophecy was not then understood by him. For, if the prophecy was commonly understood in the sense afterwards explained to him by "the Angel of the Lord," he would certainly conclude that Mary was the virgin referred to by Isaias. Knowing her as he did, and being persuaded of her heavenly purity and of her resolution to preserve her virginity, he had no doubt as to her innocence. His very perplexity is a proof of the virgin-birth of Christ. He was faced with a painful dilemma. On the one hand, in the eyes of his neighbours the approaching birth of his wife's child was a matter of joy and congratulation to them both. On the other hand, there could be no question in his mind of any suspicion of adultery.

It seems clear from the Gospel narrative that Joseph did not become aware of the pregnancy of Mary until her return to Nazareth, and it is sometimes suggested that she assumed that the consequences of her return in that condition would expose her to a painful misunderstanding. But there is nothing in the Gospel which suggests that she supposed Joseph to be in ignorance of the true fact. The angel of the Lord had come to herself with a special message, as befitted so wonderful an event; the angel had come to inform Zachary that his wife would bear him a son, and that it would be an

[2] Cf. p. 30.

occasion of "joy and gladness"; and surely Mary never doubted that God would send His angel to Joseph to tell him of the Son whom his wife had so miraculously conceived. If Zachary was to have "joy and gladness" and many to "rejoice in his (John's) nativity," surely Mary would conclude that the advent of such a Son as hers would be still more the source of joy and gladness. Even to us it would certainly appear that the absence of such a personal intimation to a man in the position of Joseph would appear. Nor is there anything in the Gospel account of the Visitation to suggest such a thought. As we have pointed out, one of the most striking features of Mary's *Magnificat* was the spirit of joy and happiness it portrays. There is, in fact, not the slightest indication that Mary did not return to Joseph and her home with every sentiment of confidence and happiness. There was no reason for her to suppose that her relatives and neighbors had any other sentiments towards her than those of sympathy and congratulation.

It is equally clear that Joseph did not know of what had taken place until Mary's return. But it is not necessary to suppose that it was only after her arrival in her home, or that it was from herself that he first received information. Many writers [3] think that the fact of the pregnancy of Mary was first observed by the women. In any case, it is probable that some one arriving shortly be-

[3] Maldonatus (Matt. i, 18) says that the words "she was found with child" are not to be taken as meaning that it was specially by Joseph, but that the fact was apparent to all. Lagrange adopts this view: "Are not women the first to notice such facts in the case of other women? But Joseph was bound to be told about it. And he was." Prat and others could be also cited.

fore Mary would have known the fact and mentioned it to Joseph by way of congratulation. It would, therefore, be probable that Joseph's perplexity and the reassurance by the angel took place before Mary entered "her house."

We do not know how long this state of perplexity lasted. À Lapide commenting on the words, "While he thought on these things," says: "Not fully coming to a conclusion: it was a first thought, and as it were a first movement of his mind." All are agreed that the angel came to him before he had come to any decision. If we are to take the words "in his sleep" in their literal sense, we may conclude that he had heard the news the day before Mary's return. In the Gospel of St. Matthew such messages are always introduced by these words. For example, Pilate's wife said to him: "Have nothing to do with that just man. For I have suffered many things this day in a dream because of him" (xxvii, 19). It may be that the angel appeared to Joseph when he was in a species of reverie, musing over what he had heard, or almost certainly in his prayer for light. His first thought was one of perplexity. There are no grounds for the view held by some—Fouard among others [4]—that Joseph suspected Mary of adultery. He knew and loved her too well to think that. But the fact was that the child was not his, no matter how much he loved her, or what explanation there might be. As a "just man," in the first place, he could not treat as guilty one whom he firmly believed to be innocent, but it was equally incumbent on him as a just man to refuse to acknowledge as his a child of an-

[4] "He was eager to repair the unmerited outrage Mary had suffered in his thoughts."—(p. 40).

other. Most of the writers dwell on his desire to protect the good name of Mary, *but do not sufficiently bring out another aspect of his justice.* Joseph was in the eyes of the people "the son of David," that is to say, the head and representative of the royal family, of which the Messiah was to be born. He knew that he would never have a son, and that the heir to David would spring from another member of that family, probably through his brother Cleophas. It would be an act of grave injustice to God and to the family of which he was the custodian to acknowledge as his heir one whom he believed to be the son of an unknown father. Thus, no matter how much he loved Mary or was convinced of Mary's innocence, and that she had possibly been the innocent victim of some outrage, he could not as a man of honour acknowledge her child as his own. It was when he was thinking over what course he would adopt which would, as far as possible, save Mary's good name and satisfy his own sense of justice that the angel came to announce to him the "great things" which God had done to Mary. Thus, his mind set at ease, knowing that he himself was the "son of David," through whom, as legal father of Mary's Son, Christ was to inherit the titles of David, he welcomed her back with that joy and gladness of which she felt assured.

This account of the perplexity of St. Joseph, and its prompt removal by the angel's words, is in harmony with the other visits of Gabriel—for it is probable that he was the messenger sent by God to Daniel, Zachary and Mary —in what concerned the Incarnation. In them all the recipients of the message were not long left in suspense, and no sooner were they "troubled" than they were reassured. The thoughts of Joseph were not revealed until St. Matthew told the story years after. Nor is there any indication in the Gospel narrative that Mary was aware at this time of the keen, if brief, agony through which the soul of Joseph passed before the angel said: "Fear not to take unto thee Mary thy wife," on her return. Why should Joseph, whose love and consideration for his wife come out so clearly in the account of his fears, tell her of these thoughts? The consideration and understanding of ordinary human nature would, in a similar crisis, forbid the infliction of so great a pain on the heart of one who is loved. Still more would the soul of a chosen one such as Joseph recoil from such an action. There is not the slightest indication in the Gospel that the joy which filled Mary's soul, as shown in her *Magnificat*, was marred by the least cloud which could overshadow the welcome which awaited her on her return home. The sword of sorrow was to come later. Joseph, no doubt, made it clear that he too had been made aware of the miraculous conception of her Child, as Mary would most confidently have anticipated.

And Joseph her husband took unto him his wife with a new love and reverence, and was united to her by a closer bond than ever. He was to be the father in the eyes of God and of men of the Son Mary had conceived of the Holy Ghost, and to be the head of that Holy Family through whom Jesus was to be known as the Son of David. St. Matthew reminds us in a Hebrew form of speech that, though truly the husband of Mary, they were united in a virgin marriage, and that as Mary had conceived as a virgin, such she would remain.

CHAPTER VI

THE DIGNITY OF JOSEPH

"Jesus . . . being (as was supposed) the son of Joseph"
(St. Luke iii, 23).

WITH the visit of the angel, the manifestation of the
mystery of the Incarnation, and the divine appointment
of Joseph as head of the Holy Family, his life entered on
a new phase. In discussing the position and dignity of
Joseph we cannot do better than follow the teaching of
Suarez,[1] who has fully examined every aspect of the subject in the section on "St. Joseph, the spouse of the
Blessed Virgin":

Joseph was the true husband of Mary:

"The first dignity of St. Joseph is that he was the
spouse of Mary, and, while being united to her in virgin-
marriage, he enjoyed all the rights and obligations of a
true spouse. If it was right for St. Gregory Nazianzenus,
wishing to praise the husband of his sister Gorgonia, to
say *"Do you wish me to describe in a word her husband?
He was her husband. Nor do I know what else it is necessary for me to say,"* in order to praise Joseph, is it not

[1] *De mysteriis vitae Christi,* Q. xxix, Art. ii, Ch. viii, sect. 1.

53

much more sufficient for us to say that he was "*The hus-band of Mary*"?

Joseph the supposed father of Christ.—How glorious *is the name: Father of Christ.*

"Hence Joseph obtained the name and estimation of being the father of Christ, as is clear from Luke iii, 23: *being as was supposed the son of Joseph;* Matt. xiii, 55: *Is not this the carpenter's son?* John vi, 42: *Is not this Jesus the son of Joseph?* As St. Augustine says, this ap-pellation was accepted not only by the people who were ignorant of the divinity and admirable conception of Christ, but also by the Evangelist and by the Blessed Virgin herself, who said: *Thy father and I have sought thee sorrowing* (Luke ii, 48). And the Evangelist says: *When his parents brought the child Jesus* (Luke ii, 22); and again: *And his father and mother were wondering at those things, which were said concerning him* (Luke ii, 33). From which we may understand that this name was not given to Joseph without the special providence of God, because neither the Blessed Virgin nor St. Luke used it without the special inspiration of the Holy Ghost. The words spoken by Jesus on the cross, *Woman, be-hold thy son,* showed the special love He had for St. John, and the dignity of the office conferred on him by substituting him for Himself in the care and love of His mother. But much more excellent is the title of "father of Christ" than that of "son of the Virgin," not only because the title of father carries with it greater authority, but also because the dignity of Christ infi-nitely surpasses that of the Virgin."

*The part of Joseph towards Christ was truly paternal.
—Joseph the guardian of Christ and of the Virgin:*

"Hence St. Joseph, while not the earthly father of Christ, enjoyed not only the name of father, but all that belongs to an earthly father. Thus he had the affection, solicitude and, so to speak, the authority of a father." As St. Bernard says: "He was the faithful and prudent servant whom God appointed to be the consoler of the mother of Christ, her bodily support, her sole most faithful coadjutor on earth in His great plan, so that not without reason that which was written about the other Joseph may be applied to him: 'He made him lord of His house and prince over all His possessions' . . ."

By adoption, even he who is altogether a stranger becomes a son, and he who adopts him is called father and, in a manner, is so; but Joseph adopted Him, whom by the sole power of the Holy Ghost Mary brought forth, and received Him as a beloved son given to him by God. . . . Unless we wish to say that Christ elected Joseph to be His father, and constituted Himself to be his Son.[2] This can also be explained in another way, for by his true marriage with the Virgin, in a certain sense he became the owner of her body. "Because (as Paul says) the

[2] "But in the opinion of the Jews a legal filiation had 'no less value than a real filiation for it conferred the same right.' Little does it matter, then, that Jesus was only the adopted son of Joseph. Joseph, by accepting Him as his own, transferred to Him all his rights to the royal succession of David. This principle was at that time so well recognized that no Jewish judge would have denied Jesus the legitimacy of His titles. It is not without good reason that St. Matthew, in concluding his enumeration, calls to mind that 'Joseph was the husband of Mary,' since the Child of the Virgin Mother would thus become the heir of His legal father."—Fillion I, Ch. iii, end.

husband is head of the wife, as Christ is head of the Church" (Eph. v, 23).[3]

Thus it is that the fruit of her virginal body belonged in a certain sense to Joseph. . . . For if a fountain were miraculously to spring up in a garden it would belong to him who owned the garden. . . . By the bond of a virginal marriage, the two become one heart and one will. So that they enjoy all things in common, so that what is under the dominion and power of one consequently in some way belongs to the other. Therefore, because the Blessed Virgin was the true mother of Christ, it was impossible for Joseph to be her true husband without participating in His parentage."

How great was the bond of love between Mary and Joseph?

"From all this we can understand that there was between Mary and Joseph, and also between Jesus and Joseph a special bond of mutual love and most perfect affection, which arose intrinsically from the dignity and state to which this man was elevated; for it belongs to the virtue and holiness of a wife that she should love

---

[3] Referring to the passage of St. Paul, "For whosoever are led by the Spirit of God, they are the sons of God. For you have not received the spirit of bondage again in fear; but you have received the spirit of adoption of sons, whereby we cry: Abba (Father). For the Spirit himself gives the testimony to our spirit that we are the sons of God. And if sons, heirs also: heirs indeed of God, and joint heirs with Christ: yet if so we suffer with him, that we may also be glorified with him" (Rom. viii, 14-17), St. Augustine, speaking of St. Joseph, says: "And it is not false to say that a son whom a man has adopted is begotten by him, not in the flesh, but by charity. For even we to whom God gave the power to become His sons, are not begotten of His nature and substance, but are only adopted in love."

her husband, and wish for and procure for him all that is good, especially for his soul. But the most Blessed Virgin was in all things most perfect; therefore she excelled also in this love. There is also the reason which springs from gratitude due to benefactors, which can be repaid by nothing better than by love. But St. Joseph suffered much, and undertook many labours for the sake of the Virgin, and, as was to be expected, did so with the greatest love and goodwill. There was also the similarity of their tastes and habits, the long daily familiarity and their life together, without any occasion for disagreement, all of which cannot but foster the highest kind of love and mutual benevolence. And these same reasons in a similar proportion apply to Christ our Lord, and the more so since He did all things more perfectly than the Virgin."

Sometimes St. Joseph is called the foster-father of Jesus. From the foregoing considerations it would appear that this title is not in accordance with the dignity of his office. A foster-father is chosen by parents or guardians. But Joseph was chosen by God Himself to be in all things a father to the Child who had no earthly father. It was his privilege not only to undertake all the duties of a father towards Jesus, but to be His legal father in the eyes of God and men. It was through Joseph that He was to trace His descent from David. It was as son of Joseph that His name was inscribed in the official registry of His birth as the Son of David. Jesus owed nothing to Joseph in His human origin, but it is clear that "Joseph the husband of Mary, of whom was born Jesus, who is called Christ," was essential to the coming of the Messiah among men in the manner decreed by God, and for his recognition as "Son of man." Henceforth, until his death, Mary and Joseph were never separated throughout the Hidden Life. It is with Joseph the initiative lies as head of the Holy Family; it is he who receives the commands of God in all that concerns their human lives.

CHAPTER VII

THE JOURNEY TO BETHLEHEM

"And Joseph also went up from Galilee out of the city of Nazareth into Judea, to the city of David, which is called Bethlehem" (St. Luke ii, 4).

"And it came to pass that in those days there went out a decree from Caesar Augustus that the whole world should be enrolled. This enrolling was first made by Cyrinus the governor of Syria. And all went to be enrolled, every one to his own city. And Joseph also went up from Galilee out of the city of Nazareth into Judea, to the city of David, which is called Bethlehem, because he was of the house and family of David, to be enrolled with Mary, his espoused wife, who was with child. And it came to pass that when they were there, her days were accomplished that she should be delivered. And she brought forth her first-born son, and wrapped Him up in swaddling clothes, and laid Him in a manger: because there was no room for them in the inn."—St. Luke ii, 1-7.

In the above passage it is of interest to note that although Mary and Joseph were married at this time, she is referred to in the Vulgate as "his espoused wife." According to the best Greek text (adopted by Lagrange, R. Knox, etc.) the word "wife" is not found, and the

reading is, "with Mary espoused to him," [1] corresponding exactly to the words of the account of the Annunciation in St. Luke: "a virgin espoused to a man whose
name was Joseph," and in St. Matthew (after the Visitation): "When his mother Mary was espoused to Joseph
. . ." St. John Chrysostom explains this as indicating that
Mary and Joseph were united by a virgin-marriage, and
that, although married, Mary was as a virgin, only espoused. This view is held by Maldonatus, and by modern
writers such as Eric Burrows and Fillion. The latter says:
"It is certainly remarkable and, if authentic, harmonises
with the idea which St. Matthew and St. Luke wish to
inspire in their readers on the subject of the perfect virginity of Mary, who was the wife of Joseph and at the
same time chaste as a bethrothed." We find the same
usage in the Church to-day. St. Joseph is always referred
to in liturgical books, such as the Roman Missal and the
Divine Office, as "Sponsus Beatæ Mariæ Virginis." It
may well be that this practice is based on apostolic tradition.

The circumstances of the birth of Jesus afford a striking instance of the workings of God's providence in
bringing about His ends through human instruments,
acting either knowingly or unknowingly in co-operation
with Him. Two parallel, but very different, series of
events secured in this case the fulfilment of the prophecy
that the Messiah was to be born in Bethlehem: "And
thou Bethlehem Ephrata, art a little one among the
thousands of Juda: out of thee shall come forth unto
me he that is to be the ruler in Israel: and his going

[1] As in the Westminster Version.

forth is from the beginning, from the days of eternity"
(Mich. v, 2). On the one hand, away in Nazareth the
great fact of the Incarnation had taken place, and in the
ordinary course it was there that the infant Jesus would
be born. There for some six months Mary was, as other
mothers, looking forward to the birth of her child, and
making all those little preparations for the great event
which occupy the loving care of every mother. It is not
for us to attempt to put in words the thoughts and
prayers and joys which filled her soul. Surely she had
much to ponder during those happy days at Nazareth
with Joseph, the sole sharer of her secret. But Nazareth
was not to be the birthplace of the Christ. For another
series of events was to bring about, through apparently
purely human means, God's design that Jesus should be
born in Bethlehem:

"And it came to pass that in those days there went
forth a decree from Cæsar Augustus; that the whole
world should be enrolled.

This enrolling was first made by Cyrinus the governor of Syria.

And all went to be enrolled, everyone to his own
city.

And Joseph also went up from Galilee out of the
city of Nazareth into Judea, to the city of David,
which is called Bethlehem: because he was of the
house and family of David,

To be enrolled with Mary his espoused wife who
was with child."

Although, according to the common Roman law, such enrolments took place at the actual place of residence of the inhabitants, in the case of the Jews their own ancient custom was observed, according to which each one registered "everyone in his own city," or place of family origin. It would appear that, to avoid confusion, there was a special time allotted for the inhabitants of every locality. This accounts for Joseph undertaking the journey in winter [2] when Mary was about to give birth to her Child. There was a special reason why Joseph should obey this decree exactly, for not only was he an exact observer of the law, but, as appears from the genealogies of St. Matthew and St. Luke, the chief representative of the royal line of David. It is not improbable that there was an obligation on women to enroll themselves; and it is also suggested that a secret inspiration induced Mary to accompany her husband, and thus fulfil the prophecy that the Messiah should be born in Bethlehem. But in any case her affection for Joseph, and the desire that he should be near her at the birth of the Child who meant so much to both, and through whom their destinies were united, was for her an imperative reason. And did she not feel the want of his sympathy and understanding? The birth of Jesus at Nazareth while Joseph was in far-away Bethlehem would, from a purely human point of view, have been inconceivable.

---

[2] "There is no reason to reject the tradition which fixes the twenty-fifth of December as the date of the Saviour's Nativity."—Fouard, p. 48.

The shepherd "deserts the heights when snow is feared in winter, and takes refuge with his sheep in some sheltering valley like that underneath Bethlehem, where the shepherds of the Nativity were keeping the night watches over their flocks."—(E. Power, *Studies*, Vol. VIII, p. 412)

Here, then, it is Joseph who undertakes the journey to Bethlehem, and it is he who takes Mary with him, since both affection and duty made it impossible for him to be separated from her who had been entrusted to his care and protection. We have to rely on tradition for many details concerning this journey. No doubt, Joseph took with him his carpenter's tools, for it would be necessary for him to find work in order to provide for the needs of Mary and himself, and for the Child about to be born. Their home would have been locked up and put under the charge of some relative. Tradition, which is supported by evidence, tells us that Our Lady was provided with an ass, and that an ox was also taken with them. This animal, no doubt, was also employed in carrying Joseph's tools and other articles, such as the mats or thin mattresses for sleep, and what would be required for the newly-born Infant. The journey would occupy about four days, so that the nights would be passed at various inns or lodgings. We are accustomed to pictures of Mary seated on the ass, which was led by Joseph. There would be nothing in their outward appearance to suggest that this simple group contained the greatest of God's treasures, and were the most beloved and privileged of the human race. Our Lady, as other Jewish women, was clothed with a blue dress and red cloak, or red dress and blue cloak, with a large white veil covering the whole body, with shoes or sandals. Joseph wore the long robe of dark colour, which served also as covering by night, for one slept in one's clothes, wrapped in the cloak on the mat or mattress referred to above.

The route taken by Mary and Joseph was most probably identical with the modern highway between Nazareth and Bethlehem, by which the motorist of to-day
may make in a few hours the journey which then required about four days. Spiritual writers ask us to dwell
with the imagination on this journey which is so full of
memories for every Christian. St. Ignatius and St. Bonaventure attached the utmost importance to visualising
as far as possible every detail of the physical surroundings
of the different events of the life of Christ. We know
from the Life of St. Ignatius that he visited some of
these places and took note of the smallest details which
might help him to bring before him the scene he wished
to "contemplate." But he did this in order that he and
others might the better understand the interior feelings
and thoughts of Jesus and those who took part in these
events. Hence the importance of endeavouring to take
part in imagination in the scene. In his brief outline of
the Nativity he tells us to consider the persons and their
thoughts, words and actions, and to recall in brief detail
the nature of the country through which they passed—
"to see with the eye of the imagination the road from
Nazareth to Bethlehem, considering its length, its
width, and whether it be level or through valleys or
over hills." I am to accompany them "as if I were there
present, making of myself a lowly and unworthy servant,
watching and contemplating them, and serving them
in their necessities with all possible eagerness and reverence."

It is in this spirit that, all through history, pilgrims

from all over the world have visited the Holy Land and brought back with them unforgettable memories. For those who have not had the happiness of enjoying such an experience, there are many excellent descriptions [3] given by those who have themselves visited these places, such as the following:

"They would have set out by the same road, about ninety miles long, which the pilgrims of to-day take about three or four days to traverse. Descending the hill of Nazareth they would have first crossed the plain of Esdraelon, all the great memories of Israel's past being aroused one after the other by the humble townships through which they passed or which lay along their route. Sulam, hallowed by Eliseus' miracles, with the *Canticle of Canticles* still echoing through its streets; Jezreel, foul with Jezebel's crimes and blood; the mountains of Gelboe, mute witnesses of the defeat and death of Saul and Jonathan; then Samaria with Hebal and Gerizim, once sacred mountains, now strongholds of Samaritan schism and hate; with Jacob's well and Jacob's tomb close to the road, as we enter the valleys' claustral depths. Then, step by step, we rise from the plain of Samaria towards the mountains of Judea. Here, to the left, are Silo and Bethel, formerly holy places of Israel, but long abandoned and rejected by God. And then at last from the heights of Scopus we see before us Jerusalem and Herod's temple, still unfinished, but already all glit-

[3] For an interesting and concise account of the Holy Land the reader is referred to *Christ's Homeland* by Rev. D. Riordan. (Gill, Dublin).

tering with marble and gold. There Almighty God still dwelt; but alas! for how long?

"To-day, no less than in the past, no pilgrim can pass unmoved across this sacred ground where God showed Himself so bountiful and man so ungrateful. But such sentiments are nothing beside the profound emotion which filled the heart of Joseph, and still more that of Mary. In these valleys and mountains the whole history of their own people lived again with its faults, prayers and hopes; and the Child that Mary bore within her had come to wash away the sins and fulfil the desires of that heroic past.

"At last they left Jerusalem behind, and after two hours on foot reached the city of David and were at home" (Lebreton, Eng. trans., p. 16).

During these days their thoughts must often have dwelt on the great events connected with the places through which they passed, and which would no doubt be subjects of conversation. But as is customary with those who are closely united by sympathy and affection, there would have been long spells of silence and prayer. Above all, Mary would have had much "to ponder over" concerning "the great things which He that is mighty had done to her," and could not but have wondered about what was to come. We can never lose sight of the fact that this was all part of God's plan for our Redemption, and the beginning of that Life which was to be lived for us. Again, to quote St. Ignatius, we are invited to "observe and consider what they are doing, as, for example, the journey and the toil in order that our Lord may be born in abject poverty, and so that after many labours, after hunger, after thirst, after heat and cold, after injuries and insults, He may die on a cross, and all this for me."

CHAPTER VIII

BETHLEHEM

"And she brought forth her first-born[1] son, and wrapped him up in swaddling clothes and laid him in a manger: because there was no room for them in the inn."

HAVING passed through Jerusalem, after a journey of two hours, Joseph and Mary reached Bethlehem. The story of the birth of Jesus is familiar to every Christian, so that it is not necessary for us to dwell on the obvious lessons of humility and unwordliness underlying the great event so simply told by St. Luke. The fact is so great that the very simplicity of the Gospel account is its most worthy description. Here again it is Mary alone who tells the story. Not only was it fitting that He who came to teach the lesson of true humility and the dignity of poverty should at the very outset give such an example, but even the whole setting of that first Christmas night would seem to demand that Christ should be born

---

[1] "In its proper meaning *prōtótokos* signifies 'first-born'—that is, *the one born first*, whether or not the first of a series. The first-born was thus called among the Jews and consecrated to God, before it was known whether he would have brothers. It is in this sense that Jesus is called the 'first-born' of Mary (Luke ii, 7)." *The Theology of St. Paul*, by F. Prat, I, p. 289.

away from the crowded town. There were many others besides Joseph who had come to Bethlehem to be registered and to pay the tax. The place was full. There were apparently no near relatives of Joseph in the town or village, and the inn, too, was full. Being poor people they had no reason to expect preference before others of their class. The fact that Mary's "days were accomplished, that she should be delivered," no doubt evoked the sympathy of the inn-keeper, who put at their disposal one of the caves or grottos which abound in this region, and which were used as a shelter for cattle.[2]

[2] There is an interesting suggestion in H. V. Morton's *In the Steps of the Master*, as to the statement that the Magi found the Child in a house: "These primitive houses in Bethlehem gave me an entirely new idea of the scene of the Nativity. They are one-room houses built over caves. Whether these caves are natural or artificial I do not know: they are level with the road, but the room above them is reached by a flight of stone steps, perhaps fifteen or twenty. The caves are used to this day as stables for the animals, which enter from the road level. There are, in most of them, a stone trough, or manger, cut from the rock, and iron rings to which the animals are tied during the night . . .

"Therefore I believe we must imagine the Nativity to have taken place in one of these old cave-houses of Bethlehem. The guest-chamber or upper room, which it was the Jewish custom to offer to travelling Jews, was evidently already occupied, and therefore the host did his best by offering the Holy Family the shelter of the downstairs room, or cave. It is interesting in this connection to remember that the ancient tradition in the Church was that Jesus was born, not in a stable or inn, but in a cave.

"Justin Martyr, who was born about 100 A.D., repeats a tradition current in his time that, as Joseph had no place in which to lodge in Bethlehem, he discovered a cave near by. But even before Justin's time, it seems that the cave below the Church of the Nativity was venerated as the scene of Christ's birth.

"Later, when the upper room was once more vacant, it would be occupied by the Holy Family. It was there that the Magi, 'entering into the house, found the child with Mary his mother, and, falling down, they adored him'; while the shepherds had 'found Mary and Joseph, and the infant lying in the manger.'"

As the story of that blessed night makes clear, in spite of the poverty and discomfort of the surroundings, the solitude and remoteness of such a place was preferable to the crowded *khan*. Such a shelter may be compared to a court surrounded by cloisters, or separate partitions open towards the centre, in one of which a family might be accommodated. The centre portion was occupied by the asses and other animals brought by the travellers; no food was provided, but there was a supply of water. The place must have been crowded by all sorts of people who, no doubt, would have spent the greater part of the night in coming and going, and was a meeting-place for relatives and friends who would have passed the night in loud talk and the usual noisy greetings. It is clear that in such a place conditions would have been even more distressing than in a grotto. In the stable there was at least peace and quietness, and a manger for the newly-born Child.

It was, therefore, with a sense of relief that Mary found herself in this grotto. Joseph would easily have procured plenty of hay or straw both for the simple couch to which Mary was accustomed, as well as for the animals which they may have brought with them. There was nothing abnormal in the presence of the ass and ox. In the descriptions of the dwellings of poor people we read that there was a raised platform on which the family slept on their mats, while the lower portion of the chamber was occupied by the animals. (Cf. Power, *Studies*, IX, p. 539.) Such a place would have been restful after the fatigue of the long journey from Nazareth. Although it is the universal belief of Catholics

that Mary, who was exempt from original sin, gave birth
to her child without pain, there is no reason to suppose
that she, any more than other mothers, was exempt from
the weariness, fatigue and discomfort of a long journey
in winter.

The actual birth of Jesus is described by St. Luke in
the simplest possible words: "And she brought forth
her first-born, and wrapped him up in swaddling clothes,
and laid him in a manger." Theologians and commentators examine at length the manner of the birth of Christ.
It is not necessary for us to follow them in the details
they treat of. All Catholics are agreed that it was miraculous. The liturgy of the Church supports the view that
Jesus was born during the night. Mary awoke to find her
Child in her arms. That she had no need of assistance is
evident from the words of St. Luke. She herself wrapped
the Infant in the swaddling-clothes she had prepared,
and laid Him on the hay or straw in the stone trough or
manger which was in the grotto. Catholic writers from
the earliest times insist that, just as after the Annunciation and the conception of Christ, Our Lady remained a
virgin in body and mind; such she remained after His
birth. In the words of St. Augustine, Mary was a virgin
ante partum, in partu et post partum—before, during
and after the birth of Jesus. There is really nothing to
add to the simple and delicate words of St. Luke.[3]

[3] It will be seen from the following passage that the care of a new-
born babe at the present time is the same as it was long before the
birth of Jesus. It is reasonable to conclude that there was no interruption of the customary procedure at the time of our Lord's birth:—
"The new-born infant is washed in warm water and well rubbed
with salt and oil by the Palestinian peasants. The rubbing is said to
strengthen the child, and is repeated the seventh day and even daily for

In the account of the birth of the Child there is no mention of Joseph, except that he was there. We may suppose that he slept near the opening of the cave wrapped up in his cloak while this wonderful event was taking place. But we cannot doubt that Mary at once awakened him to tell him the good tidings of great joy that "a child is born to us, and a son is given to us." The promise of the angel to Mary that she would bring forth a son, whom she would call Jesus . . . and who "shall be called the Son of God" was fulfilled. So too was made good the promise to Joseph that "that which is conceived in Mary thy wife is of the Holy Ghost, and she shall bring forth a son: and thou shalt call his name Jesus. For he shall save his people from their sins" (Matt. i, 20, 21).

From the moment of the Annunciation, as Mary sang in the *Magnificat*, her soul "hath rejoiced in God her Saviour." The birth of her Son is represented by the

the first week. The infant is moreover wrapped in swaddling-clothes, as was our Divine Lord after His birth. The swaddling-clothes consist of a tiny shirt, a cap, a cotton coat, and over these a long strip of calico wound tightly several times around the body, legs and arms to ensure rigidity and straightness. Over this again a large square of print or similar stuff is tightly secured. The child is kept thus 'cribbed, cabined and confined' for two or three months, and even longer if it be weak. Perhaps we can now realise better what discomfort and humiliation being wrapped in swaddling-clothes meant to our Divine Lord, and find a deeper meaning in the words of the angel to the shepherds: 'And this shall be a sign unto you. You shall find the child wrapped in swaddling-clothes and laid in a manger.' The following passage of the prophet Ezechiel implies that all these modern usages existed in his day and that they were intended to secure the health of the child; for he ascribes metaphorically to a neglect of them the moral weakness of the Jewish nation: 'And when thou wast born in the day of nativity . . . thou wast not washed with water nor salted with salt nor swaddled with clouts.' "—E. Power, S.J., *Studies*, Vol. IX, p. 399.

Evangelist as the occasion of great joy for men and angels. The whole liturgy of the Church re-echoes this joy, and every Christian at Christmas-time endeavours to recover a little of this spirit of great joy. But it would be an impertinence to attempt to put into words the unutterable joy and thanksgiving which filled the hearts of Mary, His virgin-mother, and Joseph, to whom both Mary and Jesus had been given by God as His most precious possession. These are things for us to ponder. Catholic art has always loved to depict the scene of the Nativity, but the stark realities of that first Christmas night are too often hidden by a romantic interpretation. It is before the crib that we are invited to "taste the infinite sweetness and delight of the Divinity" there Incarnate. It is not through the medium of words that the lesson of the Child in the manger, surrounded by the Virgin-mother, St. Joseph, the shepherds, and the ass and ox that knew their Master's crib, can be taught, but by the response of our own hearts to the teachings of our Faith.

"And there were in the same country shepherds watching, and keeping the night-watches over their flock. And behold an angel of the Lord stood by them, and the brightness of God shone round about them, and they feared with a great fear. And the angel said to them: Fear not; for behold I bring you good tidings of great joy, that shall be to all the people: For this day is born to you a SAVIOUR, who is Christ the Lord, in the city of David. And this shall be a sign unto you. You shall find the infant wrapped in swaddling clothes, and laid in a manger. And suddenly there was with the angel a multitude of the heavenly army, praising God, and saying: Glory to God in the highest: and on earth peace to men of good will. And it came to pass, after the angels departed from them into heaven, the shepherds said one to another, Let us go over to Bethlehem, and let us see this word that is come to pass, which the Lord hath shewed to us. And they came with haste: and they found Mary and Joseph, and the infant lying in the manger. And seeing, they understood of the word that had been spoken to them concerning this child. And all that heard wondered: and at those things that were told them by the shepherds. But Mary kept all these words, pondering them in her heart. And the shepherds returned, glorifying and praising God for all the things they had heard and seen, as it was told unto them" (St. Luke, ii, 8-20).

It was becoming that the birth of the Good Shepherd, who was the descendant of David—himself a shepherd—should first be announced to shepherds, and that He who came to be poor and to comfort the poor should first be made manifest to them. There is nothing to add to the simple and beautiful account given by St. Luke.

Here again Joseph reappears on the scene, and from now on there is no event in the infancy and childhood of Jesus in which he is not associated with Mary—"being (as was supposed) the father of Jesus." Mary, as was her wont, treasured all these things in her heart, and told them to the Evangelist as precious memories of her Child's birthday.

CHAPTER IX

THE CIRCUMCISION AND PURIFICATION

"They carried Him to Jerusalem, to present Him to the Lord" (Luke ii, 22).

"And after eight days were accomplished that the child should be circumcised, His name was called Jesus, which was called by the angel, before He was conceived in the womb.

"And after the days of her purification according to the law of Moses were accomplished, they carried Him to Jerusalem, to present Him to the Lord: as it is written in the law of the Lord, *Every male opening the womb shall be* called holy to the Lord: and to offer a sacrifice according as it is written in the law of the Lord, a pair of turtle doves, or two young pigeons. And behold there was a man in Jerusalem named Simeon, and this man was just and devout, waiting for the consolation of Israel: and the Holy Ghost was in him. And he had received an answer from the Holy Ghost, that he should not see death before he had seen the Christ of the Lord. And he came by the Spirit into the temple. And when His parents brought in the child Jesus, to do for Him according to the custom of the law, he also took Him into his arms, and blessed God, and said: Now thou dost dismiss Thy servant, O Lord, according to Thy word in peace. Because my eyes have seen Thy salvation, which Thou hast prepared before the face of all peoples: A light to the revelation of the Gentiles, and the glory of Thy people Israel. And His father and mother were wondering at those things, which were spoken concerning Him. And Simeon blessed them, and said to Mary His mother: Behold this child is set for the fall, and for the resurrection of many in Israel, and for a sign which shall be contradicted. And thy own soul a sword shall pierce, that out of many hearts thoughts may be revealed.

"And there was one Anna a prophetess, the daughter of Phanuel, of the tribe of Aser: she was far advanced in years, and had lived with her husband seven years from her virginity. And she was a widow until fourscore and four years; who departed not from the temple, by fastings and prayers serving night and day. Now she at the same hour coming in, confessed to the Lord; and spoke of Him to all that looked for the redemption of Israel." (St. Luke ii, 21-38.)

BEING like to men in all things save sin, the rite of circumcision was for Christ a necessary fulfilment of the law. This rite had a religious aspect, and was a sign of the covenant between God and man, and the child that "shall not be circumcised, that soul shall be destroyed out of his people: because he hath broken my covenant" (Gen. xvii, 14). It is generally held that this painful rite was performed by Joseph in the presence of Mary and some few witnesses, and probably in the grotto where He was born. Writers call attention to the contrast between this simple statement of St. Luke and his elaborate description of the circumcision of John the Baptist six months previously. St. Luke gives more prominence to the naming of the Child Jesus. Now for the first time could Mary and Joseph call Him *Jesus*—that name which was to mean so much to them, and the invocation of which was to work such marvels among men.

It is not for us here to recall the words of St. Bernard

and other holy writers in praise of the Holy Name, or to
trace its use by the Apostles after the death of Christ.
As we have seen, this name was revealed both to Mary
and Joseph, and to each of them were said the selfsame
words: "and thou shalt call his name Jesus" (Luke i,
31, and Matt. i, 21). It was by this name that our Lord
was known throughout His life on earth, and to-day it
is the holiest word on the lips of every true Christian.
It was Joseph who officially conferred this name on
Mary's Son—"a name that spoke of salvation to the Jews,
and recalled thoughts of their entrance into the Promised Land and of the return from captivity. The sub-
limest of the titles of the Christ—the Messiah—only
compasses in its meaning the majesty of the Son of
God, the Anointment by which He was consecrated
King and Pontiff. The name Jesus signifies One who has
loved us even to the dying for us; it bears in upon the
heart with a profounder impress of love, a celestial sweetness, a secret relish of salvation, and a foretaste of our
deliverance" (Fouard, I, p. 55). In fact, "a name that
is above all names."

It is probable that, soon after the birth of Jesus, Joseph
succeeded in obtaining a better lodging for Mary and
her Child.[1] The crowds would have dispersed, and there
would now "be room for them." In support of this view
is the statement of St. Matthew that when the Magi
came to present their gifts they found Mary with the
Child in a "house." It was here that Mary passed the
forty days which were to intervene before she came with
Joseph to present and redeem Jesus in the Temple.

[1] Cf. above, p. 71.

(Exod. xiii, 2, 12, etc.) The "first-born" boy of all Jews
was at first destined for the sanctuary, but later on this
dignity was reserved exclusively to the tribe of Levi. The
first-born sons of other tribes had to be redeemed by
the payment of what in our money was equivalent to
about 12s., which went to the Temple treasury. Jesus,
who belonged to the tribe of Juda, had therefore to be
redeemed. Another law prescribed that for the space of
forty days after the birth of a son, the mother was ob-
liged to live in retirement. At the end of that period the
mothers were to present themselves at the Temple or a
synagogue to be purified from the legal "impurities" they
had contracted by child-birth.

It is probable that this law, like others concerning
"uncleanness," had its origin in hygienic reasons, but
among the Jews they had assumed a religious character.
It was usual to combine the observation of the redemption of the child with the ceremony of the purification
of the mother, and, if possible, in the Temple of Jerusalem itself. The proximity of Bethlehem and the desire
of Joseph and Mary to carry out the law in all its exact-
ness naturally induced them to do so at the first opportunity. It is pointed out by the Fathers and theologians
that neither Mary nor Jesus could be said to come under
this law. Nevertheless, apart from their personal devotion, it is evident that Jesus being "as was supposed" the
son of Joseph as well as of Mary, could not, in the eyes
of men, be exempt from a tittle of the external observ-
ances so rigidly adhered to by all Jews.

Therefore Jesus, as belonging to the tribe of Juda,
must needs be redeemed, and Mary His mother take part

of the ceremony of purification.[2] Thus, "after the days of her purification according to the law of Moses were accomplished, they carried him to Jerusalem, to present him to the Lord." It is not clear in what the ceremony of purification consisted. It has been suggested that the priests sprinkled the mother with "lustral water," accompanied by certain prayers. The essential part of the ceremony consisted in the sacrifices, "according as it is written in the law of the Lord, a pair of turtle doves or two young pigeons" (Luke ii, 24). In the case of the rich, a lamb a year old was prescribed for one of the sacrifices. For the poor, a turtle dove or young pigeon might be substituted. It is not said which Joseph had provided. These birds could be purchased from the merchants, who, later on, attracted our Lord's indignation. In any case, the poverty of the Holy Family is made clear.

This scene brings out clearly the intimate union between Mary and Joseph, and the recognition of Joseph as father of Jesus in the sight of God and men. Every word of St. Luke's account of this event is full of meaning and deserves close study. We are to think of Mary and Joseph—who possibly carried the infant Jesus—making their way through the streets of Jerusalem and entering the Temple. Here they were met by the just and devout Simeon, a man of Jerusalem, who, under the inspiration of the Holy Ghost, was "waiting for the con-

[2] The Vulgate states that this visit took place "after the days of her (Mary's) purification according to the law of Moses were accomplished," but the majority of the MSS. use the words "their days of purification": indicating the earliest time when both parents could go together to the temple, Joseph to offer to God and redeem (by payment of five shekels) the first-born son, and Mary for her purification. (Cf. Westminster Version, Luke ii, 21, and note.)

solation of Israel," and whose prayers had been answered by "the Holy Ghost that he should not see death, before he had seen Christ the Lord." The same Spirit urged him to be in the Temple at the moment when "His parents brought the child Jesus, to do for him according to the custom of the Law." He recognised in this modest group the fulfilment of his ardent desires, and thanking God "he also took him into his arms." Then, still under the inspiration of the Holy Ghost, he uttered the short but beautiful canticle, the *Nunc Dimittis*, which, with the *Benedictus*, the *Magnificat* and the *Gloria in excelsis*, adorns the sublime memory of the Incarnation:

"Now thou dost dismiss thy servant, O Lord, according to thy word in peace.

Because my eyes have seen thy salvation,

Which thou hast prepared before the face of all peoples:

A light to the revelation of the Gentiles, and the glory of thy people Israel."

This canticle is both a *Te Deum* and a prophecy—a thanksgiving for the privilege of seeing and holding in his arms the Redeemer, the glory of His people, and a prophecy of the promised Messiah who was to save and illumine by His grace not only Israel but the whole world. In the previous messages of the Angel to Mary and Joseph, the Son promised to her was described rather as the Saviour of the Jews, and the same thought is contained in the *Magnificat* and the *Benedictus*. Here He is declared to be sent both to Jews and Gentiles. It is no wonder that "His father and mother were wondering at those things, which were spoken concerning him."

Simeon blessed both Mary and Joseph as he held the Child in his arms—the first "Benediction"! But he had a special message for the young mother who was to be so closely bound to her Son by ties of love, and what is the necessary complement of love—suffering. What was revealed to her in a vague way at the beginning of the life of Christ, in order to prepare her for what lay before her, was soon to be realised in hard fact. We, too, reading the history of Christ's life and death, realise how true were the words which fell from the lips of Simeon:

> "Behold this child is set for the fall, and for the resurrection of many in Israel, and for a sign which shall be contradicted, and thy own soul a sword shall pierce, that out of many hearts thoughts may be revealed."

Already Mary had learned that the great dignity which was hers was not exempt from trials and hardships, but this is the first direct reference to them in the Gospel story.

As Simeon was addressing Mary and Joseph, another venerable personage joined the little group. This was Anna, who was evidently an important person and is described by St. Luke as a prophetess; not because she necessarily foretold the future, but because, being inspired by God, she recognised in the Child in the arms of Simeon, the Redeemer for whose coming she had so long and ardently hoped and prayed, "and spoke of Him to all who looked for the redemption of Israel." As has been suggested, it is more than likely that she had got to know and love the young mother during the years Mary spent in the Temple, for Anna "departed not from the Temple, by fastings and prayers serving night and day." Sacred writers point out that it was fitting that the Messiah should be welcomed into His Father's house by representatives of the states of virginity, marriage and widowhood.

Such, in brief outline, was this momentous visit of Jesus, Mary and Joseph to the Temple of God. It will be noticed that the account of the Evangelist takes little heed of the rites of the actual presentation of Jesus and the purification of Mary—both of which were, in truth, but the fulfilling of the laws which evidently did not apply either to Jesus or to Mary. As this humble pair with their Infant departed to their home they had surely much to wonder at and ponder in their hearts. All unsuspected by the throngs through which they made their way, passed the Lord of Creation as a little Child carried in the arms of His parents.

St. Luke passes on at once to the life of the Holy Family at Nazareth, and omits altogether the intervening events which have been described by St. Matthew.

CHAPTER X

THE MAGI AND FLIGHT INTO EGYPT

"Joseph . . . arise and take the Child and His Mother and fly into Egypt" (Matt. i, 13).

"When Jesus therefore was born in Bethlehem of Juda, in the days of King Herod, behold there came wise men from the East to Jerusalem, saying: 'Where is He that is born King of the Jews? For we have seen His star in the East, and are come to adore him.' And King Herod, hearing this, was troubled, and all Jerusalem with him. And assembling together all the chief priests and the scribes of the people, he inquired of them where Christ should be born. But they said to him: 'In Bethlehem of Juda; for so it is written by the prophet: *And thou Bethlehem the land of Juda art not the least among the princes of Juda: for out of thee shall come forth the Captain that shall rule my people Israel.'* Then Herod privately calling the wise men learned diligently of them the time of the star which appeared to them; and sending them into Bethlehem, said: 'Go and diligently inquire after the Child; and when you have found Him, bring me word again, that I also may come and adore Him.'

"Who having heard the king, went their way; and behold the star which they had seen in the East, went before them, until it came and stood over where the Child was. And seeing the star they rejoiced with exceeding great joy. And entering into the house, they found the Child with Mary His mother, and falling down they adored Him: and opening their treasures, they offered Him gifts; gold, frankincense, and myrrh. And having received an answer in sleep that they should not return to Herod, they went back another way into their country.

"And after they were departed, behold an angel of the Lord appeared in sleep to Joseph, saying: Arise, and take the Child and His mother, and fly into Egypt: and be there until I shall tell thee. For it will come to pass that Herod will seek the Child to destroy Him. Who arose, and took the Child and His mother by night, and retired into Egypt: and He was there until the death of Herod: that it might be fulfilled which the Lord spoke by the Prophet, saying: *Out of Egypt have I called My Son.*"—(St. Matthew ii, 1-15.)

IMMEDIATELY after the account of the presentation in the Temple, St. Luke says: "And after they had performed all things according to the law of the Lord, they returned to Galilee, to their city, Nazareth." He makes no mention at all of the visit of the Magi, the massacre of the Innocents or the flight of the Holy Family into Egypt. While there are certain authors who hold that the return to Nazareth took place immediately after the Presentation, the almost unanimous view is that the Holy Family did not settle there until after their return from Egypt. It is St. Matthew who describes what took place in the interval.

The visit of the Wise Men, or Magi, is of importance in the life of Christ, in that it is the manifestation of redemption to the Gentiles, and is celebrated throughout the Church with the greatest solemnity. We need not dwell on the event in detail. The Gospel tells us the story, and there is very little that can be added to it with any certainty. Its bearing on the life of Joseph is that it was the occasion of the flight into Egypt.

There is no solid foundation for the belief that these Wise Men were kings. They came from a land where the course of the heavens was studied with almost religious reverence. Fouard says:

"Being subject to the authority of Daniel, the Magi —Chaldean as well as Persian—could not possibly have been ignorant of his predictions of a Messiah, in which he had gone so far as to mark the year, the month, and the hour of His birth. They had learned from him that the Saint of Saints, who should receive divine anointment, was that very One whom Balaam had beheld rising from Jacob like a Star (Num. xxiv, 17). From the Magi these prophecies were disseminated among the people; and in the time of Jesus there was a settled conviction, cherished likewise throughout all the East, that a King was to arise from Judea, who should conquer the world.

"In the midst of this expectancy a strange Star shone out suddenly in the Eastern sky. The Magi always followed the course of the stars attentively; in the clear nights of the Orient, when the heavens hang out all their glittering lamps, they had remarked this star, and recognised it as the signal for some great marvel. And at the same time their hearts as well as their eyes were opened to admit the light which heralded the Christ; they recalled to each other the Star of Jacob and of Judea, and three from among them resolved to travel afar in search of Him of whose approach the heavens were telling" (Vol. I, Ch. v.)

With regard to the text of St. Matthew, it is to be noted that his words imply that the visit of the Magi took place soon after the birth of Jesus, and in Bethlehem. They found the Child with Mary His mother "in the house" which Joseph's care had provided for them as soon as the crowds had dispersed. There is no mention of Joseph's presence at the actual time of the arrival of the Magi, but that does not imply his absence. Indeed, since, as we believe, St. Matthew derived his knowledge of these events, at least indirectly, from Joseph himself, is it not reasonable to suppose that he described the scene as he had beheld it? The charming picture of the young mother with the Child in her arms, before whom the Magi in their bright robes were prostrate in adoration and offering their treasures, was one which would remain for ever in his memory. Joseph himself did not come into the picture.

But this visit of the Magi who came to adore Him "that is born King of the Jews" had serious consequences for Joseph and his family and for many besides. The Magi did not return to bring word to Herod, for "having received an answer in sleep that they should not return to Herod, they went back another way into their country." Herod was not one who would tolerate a rival King, and he would stop at nothing to remove Him. The delusion practised on him by the Wise Men constituted an immediate danger for the newly-born Child:

"And after they departed, behold an Angel of the Lord appeared in sleep to Joseph, saying: Arise, and take the child and his mother, and fly into Egypt; and be there until I shall tell thee. For it will come to pass that Herod will seek the child to destroy Him. Who arose, and took the child and his mother by night, and retired into Egypt."

Here again we find Joseph acting as head of the Holy Family. It was he who "went up from Galilee" bringing Mary with him, so that Jesus might be born in Bethlehem, thus being the instrument for the fulfilment of the prophecy. So too, as St. Matthew points out, it was through him "that it might be fulfilled which the Lord spoke by the prophets, saying: *Out of Egypt have I called my son.*"

Although the Christ was God, and could have escaped, by miraculous means, the dangers which threatened his life so often, we find that he took the ordinary precautions to escape from His enemies until His time was come. Just as now we find Him, at the beginning of His life, flying from Herod through the care of Mary and Joseph, so we see Him during His last year taking all human means to save Himself from His enemies—until His time had come. Already the prophecy of Simeon was being fulfilled: "Behold this child is set for the fall and resurrection of many in Israel, and for a sign which shall be contradicted, . . ."; for Herod "sending, killed all the men-children that were in Bethlehem, and in all the borders thereof, from two years and under, according to the time which he had diligently inquired of the wise men. Then was fulfilled that which was spoken by Jeremias the prophet, saying: *A voice in Rama was heard, lamentation and great mourning; Rachel bewailing her children, and would not be comforted, because they are not."*

It was evident that Joseph had to act promptly. Mary and the Infant were roused from their sleep and, with their poor belongings hurriedly collected, Joseph took them away. Again Mary had to experience the inconvenience and hardships of a hurried journey, this time into an unknown country, and with her new-born Infant to care. A few days would be sufficient to enable the Holy Family to reach the frontiers of Egypt, where they were safe from Herod. It may be said that we know nothing definite about their stay in Egypt. The picturesque accounts of the fall of idols as they passed along may be ignored, together with other wonders. As a matter of probability we may suppose that they settled down in some place where there was a Jewish settlement, or at least a number of their race. Here Joseph would have found work to provide for the support of Mary and Jesus. Our object here is not to suggest the lessons which are to be drawn from this event, or the thoughts which would have filled the minds of Mary and Joseph.

The Gospels do not tell us how long the exile lasted. Conjectures ranging from a few months to as long as nine years have been made. If, accepting the authority of the more modern Lives of Christ, we are to follow the Gospel account closely, and to suppose that the movements of Joseph followed immediately or soon after the events recounted by St. Matthew, the succession of events would be this: Herod died a few months after the massacre of the Innocents. He died of a repulsive and horrible disease, which is described at length by Jo-

sephus. It is sufficient here to say that the corruption of
the grave devoured him while still alive. Hated by all,
and cruel to the end, he caused his own son to be exe-
cuted five days before his death, and in order that tears
should accompany his corpse to the grave, ordered that
members of the chief Jewish families should be mur-
dered at the hour of his death—an order which was not
carried out.

St. Matthew tells us that when Herod was dead, an
Angel of the Lord appeared to Joseph in Egypt and told
him to take the Child and His Mother and return to
Israel, since those who sought the death of the Child
were dead. Joseph acted promptly, and brought his precious charges into Israel. From the words of the Gospel
it seems to be clear that there was no delay. St. Matthew,
who was always desirous to show how events were the
fulfilment of prophecies, says of the sojourn and return
of the Holy Family, "that it might be fulfilled which the
Lord spoke by the prophet, saying: *Out of Egypt have I
called my son.*" It would seem that Joseph did not know
at the time who was the successor of Herod—a strong
argument in favour of assigning a short period to the
exile in Egypt, for details of the death of such a king as
Herod would have spread rapidly, and especially among
the Jews.

CHAPTER XI

THE INFANCY AND CHILDHOOD AT NAZARETH

"Joseph, arise, and take the Child and His Mother and go into the land of Israel" (Matt. ii, 20).

"But when Herod was dead, behold an angel of the Lord appeared in sleep to Joseph in Egypt, saying: 'Arise, and take the Child and His mother, and go into the land of Israel, for they are dead that sought the life of the Child.' Who arose, and took the Child and His mother, and came into the land of Israel. But hearing that Archelaus reigned in Judea in the room of Herod his father, he was afraid to go thither: and being warned in sleep retired into the quarters of Galilee. And coming he dwelt in a city called Nazareth: that it might be fulfilled which was said by the prophets: That he shall be called a Nazarite."—St. Matthew ii, 19-23.)

HEROD was succeeded by Herod's son, Archelaus, later confirmed in his heritage by the Roman Emperor, not as king but as Ethnarch, or administrator subject to Rome. This man rivalled his father in cruelty, and would be as hostile to the thought of a supposed claimant to his throne as was Herod himself. Joseph would naturally return to Nazareth by the way he came, passing through Bethlehem and Jerusalem on the way. "But hearing that Archelaus reigned in Judea in the room of Herod his father, he was afraid to go thither." Some writers hold that Joseph's original intention was to settle permanently in Bethlehem, and that the return to Nazareth was due to a change of plan. But there does not seem to be any convincing argument in favour of this view. The determination to avoid Jerusalem seems to have been due to Joseph's prudence and anxious care of the charge committed to him. "Being warned in sleep he retired into the quarters of Galilee." Joseph therefore selected a safer route, probably the road along the coast, to return to their home in Nazareth, which they had left four or five months previously.

St. Matthew tells us that after the sojourn in Egypt Joseph "took the child and his mother, and came into the land of Israel . . . and coming he dwelt in a city called Nazareth." Then, as is the custom with St. Matthew, he sees in this the fulfilment of that "which was said by the prophets: that he shall be called a Nazarite." St. Luke also tells us that "after they had performed all things according to the law of the Lord, they returned into Galilee, to their city Nazareth. And the child grew, and waxed strong, full of wisdom: and the grace of God was in Him."

For convenience we may divide these hidden years of our Lord's life into two periods, separated by the Finding in the Temple, when He was twelve years old. According to the view of the best authorities, the return of the Holy Family to Nazareth took place when the Infant Jesus was some months old. We are given no details as to the life led by the Child and His parents. That our Lord's growth was externally in all things the same as that of other children is certain, and therefore His babyhood ran the ordinary course. The Gospel tells us nothing more about the infancy of Jesus beyond what is contained in the words, "the Child and His mother and Joseph"; and there is no need for anything more. Mary was the perfect mother, who devoted herself to her Child, nourishing Him, caring Him, and in all things setting the example and standard for all mothers.

To describe in detail such a motherhood would be nothing more than to attempt to put into words what had better be left to our human hearts. Apart from the miraculous conception and birth of her Son, everything goes to show that Mary had all the joys and trials incidental to motherhood. Indeed, when we consider the hardships of the winter journey from Nazareth to Bethlehem, the circumstances of the Nativity, the journey to Egypt, the sojourn there, and the journey from Egypt back to Nazareth, it does not require much imagination to realise our Lady's part, even though sustained by the love of her Child, the comfort and affection of Joseph, and, above all, by her love and trust in God. It was, then, with great joy and relief that the Holy Family found themselves once more in "their own city"—in the quiet and peaceful home of Nazareth. During these early days we picture Mary fully occupied with her Child and her household duties, and Joseph once more back at work to support those he loved so well.

We need not dwell on these years of our Lord's bodily growth, which in every way resembled that of other children. But there is an aspect of the early life of the God-Man which cannot be passed over, and which presents no little difficulty. St. Luke tells us that the "Child

grew and waxed strong, full of wisdom; and the grace of
God was in Him"; and, later on, after the finding of
Jesus in the Temple, he tells us that "Jesus advanced in
wisdom and age and grace with God and man." The
common teaching of theologians is that this wisdom, although possessed by Jesus in its fulness from the instant
of His conception, only showed itself by degrees. It is
not difficult to admit that the experimental knowledge
acquired through the senses increased in our Lord as
in all other men—even though he already possessed all
knowledge since He enjoyed the Beatific Vision and possessed infused knowledge. But since He was, in the
words of the Athanasian Creed, "perfect man as well as
perfect God," His growth in His human nature was similar to that of other men. The Infant Jesus did not simply "pretend" to be a child, but actually was one.

Our Lord as God possessed all possible knowledge,
but not as man. From the beginning of His human
life Christ had very great knowledge —all that was suitable to His position as Head and Ruler of all men and
angels—by the Beatific Vision and infused knowledge.
He had this knowledge not only in the habitual state,
but had actual use and exercise of it, i.e., mental activity
even before He came "to the use of reason." The exercise of these supernatural miraculous kinds of knowledge is independent of the physical evolution of the
brain. But He really acquired a new *kind* of knowledge—
experimental knowledge—through the senses and mental
activity extrinsically dependent on them, of many (not
of all) the things He knew by other kinds of knowledge. The acquiring and use of this kind of knowledge

was dependent on the physical evolution of the brain, and corresponded to the stages of the Child's growth. And He lived His *outward* life at Nazareth according to the growth of this knowledge, and so He "grew in wisdom" really and not in appearance only.

Therefore, while firmly believing that Jesus was God, we may see Him as a human child in the arms of His mother, and needing all the care and attention due to childhood. The greatest artists and poets have loved to portray the Madonna, the Holy Family, Jesus in the arms of Joseph. Indeed it may be said that no subject has so profoundly inspired and influenced Christian art. It would be presumptuous—even if it were possible—to describe the mutual love of these holy souls. The hymns of the Office of the Holy Family give a lovely picture of the happiness of the home at Narazeth—"No happier home than that of God." It will suffice to quote the Vesper hymn:

> "O blessed light from Heaven inclined,
> Supreme desire of all mankind,
> Jesu, whom e'en on lowly earth
> Sweet home-love greeted at Thy birth.
>
> Fair maiden Mary, full of grace,
> Maid who alone of all our race
> Couldst in chaste womb thy Jesus bear,
> Mingling thy milk with kisses rare;
>
> And thou, from holy men of old
> The Virgin's chosen ward enrolled;

Who the sweet name of Father heard
From baby lips of God the Word." [1]

We are then to see Jesus growing up from infancy to boyhood according to the ways of human nature. His natural character developed with His age and growth. There is nothing to add to the words of the Gospel that He increased in wisdom and age and grace with God and men. At every stage of this advance He was in all things the perfect child and boy as He was later the perfect man. The beauty and attractiveness of Mary's Son is something to ponder, but not to attempt to describe in words.

Jesus, as we have said, progressed as other children, and this fact brings the part played by Mary and Joseph into the picture. The influence of a mother during the early years of her Son's life is perhaps, after the grace of God, the most powerful factor in the formation of his character. Jesus, who had within Himself all that was necessary to His perfect development into manhood, nevertheless allowed Himself to be "trained" in outward behaviour by Mary and Joseph; He was "subject to them": that is to say, He not only obeyed them but was in His external life influenced by their example and characters, and fell in with their ways of life. As in the case of other children, His very accent and mode of speech would have been theirs. This would have been especially true of Mary's influence. As he grew up, the family resemblance would have doubtless become more marked. Jesus was "like" Mary, because she was His

[1] Translation of Roman Breviary. Winter Part, p. 430.

mother and the one from whom alone He derived His
human nature. He would also, no doubt, have resembled
Joseph, not on account of direct descent, but because he
was from the same stock as Mary and, as we have seen,
very closely related to her. St. John Damascene calls attention to this likeness of Jesus to Mary.

As Jesus became older it was Mary's part to help Him
in His first steps, and in His first words. She would
have taught Him to say His prayers and, as time
went on, to read and write. The Jews had no literature
but the Bible, and it was the mother's part to teach her
child the first lessons in that book, which meant so much
to Him. Joseph too would have added his knowledge
of all that would interest and be suitable for a growing
boy. Jesus responded to these lessons with the readiness
and intelligence of His wonderful soul and mind; but
there is no reason to suppose that the miraculous had
part in His education. He passed from these first lessons
to the school of the synagogue, where, we may be sure,
His teachers were delighted with this pupil who possessed every grace of body and soul joined to unsur-
passed intelligence. At school Jesus would have mixed
and played with other boys, and returned home to Mary
and Joseph; but it is really unnecessary to attempt to
describe in detail these early years. It would, indeed, be
presumptuous to do so. All authorities insist on the
mother's part in the training and education of her son:

"There could not be a national history, nor even
romance, to compare with that by which a Jewish
mother might hold her child entranced. And it was

his own history—that of his tribe, clan, perhaps family; of the past, indeed, but yet of the present, and still more of the glorious future. Long before he could go to school, or even synagogue, the private and united prayers and domestic rites, whether of the weekly Sabbath or of festive seasons, would indelibly impress themselves on his mind. In mid-winter there was the festive illumination of each home. In most houses on the first night only one candle was lit, the next two, and so on to the eighth day. Next came, in earliest spring, the merry time of *Purim*, the Feast of Esther and of Israel's deliverance through her, with its good cheer and boisterous enjoyments. Although the Passover might call the rest of the family to Jerusalem, the rigid exclusion of leaven during the whole week could not pass without its impressions. As autumn seared the leaves, the Feast of the New Year spoke of casting up of man's accounts in the great Book of Judgment, and the fixing of destiny for good or for evil. Then followed the Feast of Atonement, with its tremendous solemnities, the memory of which could never fade from mind or imagination; and, last of all, in the week of the Feast of Tabernacles, there were the strange leafy booths in which they lived and joyed, keeping their harvest-thanksgiving, and praying and longing for the better harvest of a renewed world." [2]

The part of Joseph in the education of Jesus appears from the following passage:

[2] Edersheim: *Life and Times of the Messiah*, I, Bk. ii, Ch. ix, pp. 228-230.

"But while the earliest religious teaching would, of necessity, come from the lips of the mother, it was the father who was 'bound to teach his son.' To impart to the child knowledge of the Torah conferred as great spiritual distinction, as if a man had received the Law itself on Mount Horeb. . . . Directly the child learned to speak, his religious instruction was to begin—no doubt with such verses of Holy Scripture as composed that part of the Jewish liturgy as correspond to our Creed. Then would follow other passages from the Bible, short prayers and select sayings of the sages. Special attention was given to the culture of the memory, since forgetfulness might prove as fatal in its consequences as ignorance or neglect of the Law. Very early the child must have been taught what might be called his birthday-text—some verse of Scripture beginning, or ending, with, or at least containing the same letters as his Hebrew name. This guardian promise the child would insert in his daily prayers. The earliest hymns would be the Psalms, for the days of the week, or festive Psalms, such as the *Hillel*, or those connected with the festive pilgrimages to Zion."

The regular instruction began at the age of five or six, when every child went to school.

"The children were gathered in the synagogues or school-houses, where at first they either stood, teacher and pupils alike, or else sat on the ground in a semicircle, facing the teacher. . . . The introduction of benches or chairs was of later date; but the principle was always the same, that, in respect of accommodation, there was no distinction between teacher and taught. . . . Roughly classifying the subject of study, it was held that, up to the age of ten, the Bible exclusively should be the text-book; from ten to fifteen the Mishnah, or traditional law; after that age the student should enter on those theological discussions which occupied time and attention in the higher academies of the Rabbis."

From such an account, though inferring the later period, we may form some concept of the conditions under which our Lord advanced in age and wisdom and grace with God and man. We can gather from the Gospels certain indications of the extent to which they apply to Jesus. No doubt, as He grew older He began to learn from Joseph the elements of his trade as carpenter, and to help him in his work.

Our Lord did not frequent the academies of the Rabbis, which were at Jerusalem. Had He been known there, the scene of the Finding in the Temple would not have been worded as it is in the Gospel. His education probably ended about His twelfth year. It is evident from the Gospels that He had studied the Scriptures and, of course, understood them as no other ever could. Our Lord's language was the Aramaic, but he used Hebrew and Greek at times. It is pointed out that His cousins, SS. James and Jude, each wrote an epistle in the latter tongue. As a boy and man He was a keen student of men and the world in which they and He lived. We have only to read the Gospels to realise how the smallest facts afforded Him illustrations of the doctrines He

preached. The flowers of the field and the birds of the
air reminded Him of the goodness and providence of
God. Evidently He was well acquainted with the habits
of tradesmen and the ways of commerce. It would, in
fact, be matter for a special study to enumerate the in-
stances given in the Gospels of Christ's knowledge of
the world He lived in.[3]

[3] Cf. *e.g.* Fillon.

CHAPTER XII

JESUS IS FOUND IN THE TEMPLE

"Thy father and I have sought thee sorrowing" (Luke ii, 48).

"And the Child grew, and waxed strong, full of wisdom: and the grace of God was in Him. And His parents went every year to Jerusalem at the solemn day of the pasch. And when He was twelve years old, they going up into Jerusalem according to the custom of the feast, and having fulfilled the days, when they returned, the Child Jesus remained in Jerusalem; and his parents knew it not. And thinking that He was in the company, they came a day's journey, and sought Him among their kinsfolk and acquaintance. And not finding Him, they returned into Jerusalem, seeking Him. And it came to pass, that after three days they found Him in the temple sitting in the midst of the doctors, hearing them and asking them questions. And all that heard Him were astonished at His wisdom and His answers. And seeing Him they wondered. And His mother said to Him: Son, why hast Thou done so to us? Behold Thy father and I have sought Thee sorrowing. And He said to them: How is it that you sought Me? did you not know that I must be about My Father's business? And they understood not the word that He spoke unto them.

"And He went down with them, and came to Nazareth: and was subject to them. And His mother kept all these words in her heart. And Jesus advanced in wisdom and age, and grace with God and men."—(St. Luke ii, 40-52.)

THE Gospel's silence concerning the details of the Hidden Life is broken only once—to tell us of an incident connected with what was possibly our Lord's first visit to the Temple since He was presented as an infant. The text of St. Luke does not, however, exclude the view that Jesus may have previously accompanied His parents when they went to celebrate the Passover at Jerusalem. Indeed, it seems more probable that He went with them before the incident here recorded:

> "And his parents went every year to Jerusalem, at the solemn day of the pasch.
> And when he was twelve years old, they going up to Jerusalem according to the custom of the feast.
> And having fulfilled the days, when they returned, the child Jesus remained in Jerusalem; and his parents knew it not."

The fact that St. Luke states the exact age of Jesus is not without its significance, and throws a good deal of light on the inner meaning of the incident. According to the Jewish usage, at the completion of His thirteenth year a boy became a "son of the precept" or "son of the law," and was henceforth subject to all the prescriptions of the Mosaic law, which included fasting and pilgrimages to the Temple. As we might say, he "came of age." This visit may have been made to accustom Jesus to His future visits to Jerusalem.

At the conclusion of "the days of the feast," Joseph and Mary joined the group of those who were returning to Galilee and Nazareth. They were not alarmed that Jesus was not with them. They took it for granted that

He had joined a group of friends or relations. His conduct had never caused them the slightest uneasiness. The
beginning even of the most disciplined march is one of
apparent confusion, which only gradually becomes or-
derly:

> "One must witness the setting out of an Oriental
> caravan to form an idea of the confusion which
> reigns at the time. Various groups form and break
> up. It is all a pell-mell of men, women, children, and
> beasts of burden; there are deafening shouts of peo-
> ple calling out and looking for one another; there is
> a noisy, bustling going to and fro. The departure
> is finally accomplished. Many women and old men
> ride out on asses; the other men and young people
> go on foot. A hundred incidents delay or accelerate
> the pace of the caravan. Children who at first were at
> their father's or mother's side, presently join some
> group of friends or neighbours" (Fillion, Bk. II,
> Ch. I).

But when the afternoon was passing into evening
and Jesus had not rejoined them, His parents began to
be anxious. As we have seen in the account of the flight
into Egypt, they did not consider themselves exempt
from taking the ordinary human means for safeguard-
ing their precious charge. They perhaps recalled the
fact that there were still those who sought to kill Him.
We need no more than the brief words of St. Luke to
enable us to picture their distress and anxious search.
"And thinking he was in the company, they came a
day's journey, and sought Him among their kinsfolk

and acquaintance. And not finding Him, they returned into Jerusalem, seeking him." We can picture to ourselves that painful journey; asking those whom they met about Him, always to be told that He had not been seen. Mary and Joseph would have reached the city late on that evening. The whole of the next day was spent in looking for Him, probably among friends and kinsfolk. It is perhaps surprising that they did not visit the Temple until the morning of the third day, when their sorrow was turned into joy: ". . . they found him in the temple, sitting in the midst of the doctors, hearing them and asking them questions." They saw their beloved Son, sitting, after the manner of pupils, on the floor of one of the many halls which were ranged round the main building. Artists have loved to depict the beautiful, intelligent face, lighted up with interest and understanding, as He conversed with these men, well versed in the Scriptures, concerning all which He Himself came to fulfil. No doubt the group around Him gradually increased, as the word went round that so brilliant a youth was among them, for "all that heard him were amazed at the intelligence of his answers."

It was on such a scene the eyes of Mary and Joseph rested. They looked on with wonder. They were astonished to find Jesus, always so modest and retiring, now in the midst of such a group, as we might say "holding his own" with such brilliance, and evidently attracting much attention and admiration. No doubt His mother waited until some chance interruption gave her an opportunity of addressing Him. It is to be noted that these are the first recorded words of Mary to any hu-

man being. This is also true of the reply of Jesus. As a
matter of fact, the Gospels give us no account of the
intimate family life of the Holy Family. No word at
all of Joseph is recorded. These are matters which need
no mention, and are best left to our own sympathy
and understanding.

"And seeing him they wondered; and his mother
said to him: Son, why hast thou done so to us?
Behold, thy father and I have sought thee sorrowing.

"And he said to them: How is it that you sought
me? Did you not know that I must be about my
Father's business.

"And they understood not the word that he spoke
unto them."

If those who knew Him best, and who were aware
of His divine origin, failed to grasp the full meaning of
His conduct, it is not surprising that commentators
have difficulty in explaining them simply. It is evident
that Our Lady's words referred to the fact that He had
remained behind in Jerasulem without giving them any
hint of His intention. His action could not be attrib-
uted to any neglect or want of realisation of the pain
which would be inflicted on these two hearts, which
beat in unison with His own. Our Lord's reply is at
once a justification and explanation of His action. If
Mary's words suggest a complaint that He has not
respected their feelings, His words were a mild re-
proach that they ought to have concluded that only the
highest motive would have urged Him. Possibly too His
conduct might have been a warning that, now that He

had reached the age of manhood, he must hencefor-
ward be prepared to be guided by His heavenly Father's
will rather than by His earthly parents. Two transla-
tions of the words of Jesus are justified by different
versions. The words He used, according to the Syriac
and Armenian texts, supported by the authority of
many early Fathers, may be translated: "Knew ye not
that I must needs be in my Father's house?" (Westminster Version). The more common form, "my
Father's business," is the translation of the Vulgate,
which was preferred by the western Fathers and inter-
preters. This meaning indeed would seem to be preferable, as being more easily applicable to our Lord's
action taken as a whole, including not only the fact that
He was to be looked for in the Temple, but that he had
remained behind in Jerusalem.

In our attempts to interpret the words of the Gospels
we sometimes forget to apply an obvious truth. How
different is the effect produced by the mere reading of
a play, for example, from seeing it acted by one who
lives the part and whose manner and intonation supply
what cannot possibly be expressed in print! This is all
the more true of the writers of the Scriptures, whose
well-known economy of words leaves so much to the
imagination and understanding of the reader. A smile, a
look, the stress on a single word so completely transforms the meaning of a passage in a book, when
spoken, as to produce an effect quite other than that
suggested by the cold, lifeless words of the text. When
Our Lady "pondered" the words and actions of our
Lord, she did so in the light of the surroundings and

of every detail of the Living Voice, who spoke not only by words but with every gesture, look and intonation which she treasured in her heart. This is why the masters of the spiritual life insist so strongly on the need not only of reading the Gospels but of meditating on them with deep attention. We may, then, be sure that there was no want of affection or filial devotion in this first manifestation by Jesus of the Father's paramount claim on His and their obedience to His will. The time for a more complete understanding of His divine mission was not to come until twenty years later. In the meantime His life was to be passed in the complete obscurity of a home life, which was to teach a lesson of enormous importance to mankind, and in which Mary and Joseph were also, in their degree, to increase in grace and wisdom. If He was subject to them in many things, they were still more subject to Him in all that is implied in their intimate association with the Source of all knowledge and love of God.

CHAPTER XIII

THE HIDDEN LIFE

"And he went with them, and came to Nazareth; and was subject to them" (Luke ii, 51).

AFTER the return of the Holy Family to Nazareth almost twenty years were to elapse before Jesus began His public life. All we are told of Him during these years is contained in the above few words of Luke.

Since Christ was like us in all things except sin, we must accept it as a fact that His life was in conformity with the state of life adopted by Him. It is clear from the surprise of His relatives when He first began to show forth His knowledge and miraculous powers that during these years His life in the sight of men was an ordinary one. The implication underlying the words of St. Luke is that our Lord grew up under the influences of the surroundings amidst which He lived. Chief among these were the love and care of Mary and Joseph. Not only were they chosen by God for their high office, and endowed with all the necessary qualities it demanded, but they themselves were insensibly influenced by their intimate association with Jesus, whose every word and action His mother and, doubtless, Joseph also, kept in their hearts. It was not without a deep purpose that Jesus passed so long a period of His life amid all the influences and activities which are included in "family life." For the family was designed by God to be the keystone of the whole edifice of human society. When St. Luke tells us that Jesus was "subject to" His parents, he meant not only that He obeyed them as becomes a good son, but also that in His outward life He exercised moral virtues dependently on the knowledge He acquired through the influence of His surroundings, among which the most powerful would be the "education" of family life.

We have already considered the part of Mary in the earlier years of Christ's childhood, during which Son and Mother were so much thrown together. This influence of Mary did not cease when Jesus was passing from boyhood to manhood, but was to a greater degree supplemented by that of Joseph. Perhaps the one detail of the life of the Holy Family of which we may be certain is that Jesus and Joseph were carpenters. "Is not this the carpenter's son?" was asked about Him when He first began to teach. This phrase suffices to fix the condition of life of the Holy Family. The fact that a man exercised a trade would not, in those days, necessarily indicate that such was his means of livelihood, for in every station of life manual labour was enjoined on all, however learned or wealthy. But from the whole Gospel story it is clear that Joseph supported himself and his family by his trade. Both in Greek and Latin the words, which we usually associate with working in wood, may apply to one who is either a wood or iron worker, or who works in both. In a small country town like Nazareth most of the work of a carpenter would be in wood, but would, as we find to-day, involve a knowledge of ironwork.

From this fact alone we can, without any subtle reasoning, arrive at certain conclusions which help us to visualise the kind of life spent by Jesus and His parents. It is a fact of experience that an industrious tradesman of even average ability can support his family in reasonable comfort and prosperity. That Joseph was such a man we know. The very fact of his being known as "the carpenter" would indicate that he was well known and esteemed in his trade. It is then reasonable to conclude with so many writers and commentators that the Holy Family was, if poor, in sufficiently easy circumstances.

We are therefore to represent to ourselves the family of Joseph the carpenter of Nazareth as living in the midst of their neighbours, distinguished from others only in the holiness of their lives and their love for all. It is clear from the Gospels that they had many relatives, but there does not seem to be any necessity to suppose, as some have suggested, that any of these relatives resided with them in the same house. Jesus was naturally the central interest of the lives of Mary and Joseph. The members of that family were united to each other, not only by their love of God, but also by the ties of natural affection. St. Francis de Sales, in his great *Treatise on the Love of God*, has a chapter on "How, while the whole heart is employed in sacred love, yet one may love God in various ways, and also many other things together with Him." In the section

dealing with "Loving God above all things," he has the
following paragraph, which has an application here:

"Yea, even Jacob who was called in Daniel the
holy one of God, and whom God declares Himself
to have loved, protests that he had served Laban with
all his strength, and why did he serve Laban but to
obtain Rachel, whom he loved with all his strength?
He serves Laban with all his strength, he serves
God with all his strength, he loves God with all his
strength: yet withal he loves not Rachel as God, nor
God as Rachel; he loves God as his God, above all
things and more than himself; he loves Rachel as
his wife and above all women, and as himself. He
loves God with an absolutely and sovereignly supreme love, and Rachel with a supreme nuptial love.
Nor is one love contrary to the other, since that of
Rachel does not violate the privileges and sovereign
prerogatives of the love of God." (Book X, ch. 3).

Mary and Joseph were united by a purer and deeper
natural affection in their virgin-marriage than were ever
any other husband and wife. Mary loved Jesus, and He
loved her as no other mother and son loved each other.
Jesus loved Joseph, whom from His birth He had
looked on as His father, with a greater love than son
ever had for an earthly father; and Joseph loved Jesus,
not only for Himself and because God had given Him
to his care and affection, but also because He was the
Son of Mary his beloved wife. But it is better to follow
the reticence of the Evangelists, who leave to our own

hearts and understanding all that concerns the private lives of the members of the Holy Family.

It is stated in so many words that Jesus was Himself a carpenter, and such is the constant tradition of Christianity: "Is not this the carpenter, the son of Mary . . . ?" (Mark vi, 3). It is clear that Jesus would have learned His trade from Joseph, and that therefore these two must have been thrown much together. As is usual in the East, the workshop is generally situated at some distance from the dwelling-place. While Jesus and Joseph were at work, Mary would be at home attending to her household duties, which, though simple, were enough to give her plenty of occupation. In addition to the ordinary details of housework, such as cooking and the rest, it would be for her to grind the corn for the making of bread. In those days spinning and weaving cloth were also part of women's work. Just as she made the clothes of Jesus as an infant, so now she looked after the clothing of Jesus and Joseph, and almost certainly made the seamless robe of Jesus. But Christian art also likes to depict Our Lady sitting in the workshop while the others were at work.

As to the nature of the work of Joseph and his assistant, we must assume that it was of the kind we should expect in a country village. There would be farm implements to make and repair, posts to support the roofs of dwelling-houses, doors to be made and fitted, and similar tasks. We have to remember that our Lord took on Himself the limitations of His human nature and His earthly condition of life. He who would have excelled in any and every sphere of life, chose to confine Himself to the limitations imposed by the circumstances of His state of life. The thing we may be sure of is that whatever task He undertook was carried out with the utmost perfection, and "with all His might." As the assistant of Joseph it would have been part of His duty to accompany Joseph when the work took him outside the workshop, to go on messages, and, as the years went on, to undertake such work Himself. It is hardly necessary to remark that there was often need of the greatest patience and self-control in dealing with unreasonable and inconsiderate persons. The hidden life not only teaches the worker the dignity of manual labour, but reminds the employer to respect the dignity of the worker. It is often rightly said that the best indication of the character of anyone is gained by observing how he—or she—behaves towards those who are employed. We need not here discuss all the lessons to be learned from the mysteries of the hidden life of the Holy Family. They were in brief: the perfect carrying out of the will of God, love of the neighbour in its truest sense, and perfect uprightness and honesty in their dealings with all, thus setting a standard to be aimed at by all families.

Since we are here concerned chiefly with what concerns Joseph, we must resist the temptation to follow closely the progress of Jesus from boyhood to manhood, except in so far as it helps us to understand what kind of man was St. Joseph. It would seem that Joseph was well known throughout the towns and villages of the surrounding country. When Jesus first began to teach, St. Matthew says of Him:

"And coming into his own country, he taught them in their synagogues, so that they wondered and said: How came this man by his wisdom and miracles? Is not this the carpenter's son?" (xiii, 54).

It would appear from these words that Joseph was known in other places than Nazareth not only as a carpenter but also as the father of Jesus, and seems to have had friends in Capharnaum; for, after His discourse in the snyagogue of that town, the Jews said: "Is not this Jesus the son of Joseph, whose father and mother we know?" (John vi, 42).

CHAPTER XIV

THE ·EDUCATION OF JESUS

"And Jesus advanced in wisdom and age, and grace with God and men." (Luke ii, 52).

IF it is true that Jesus came on earth to bring all men to God, clearly it is especially true of Mary and Joseph, who were bound to Him by so many ties. It was through Him that they too were to come to the Father. During these years of constant association with Jesus, both these holy souls, according to the measure of grace given to each of them, gradually grew in sanctity and union with God, and became in every way Christlike. The influence exerted by Jesus on His parents was both indirect and direct. Indirect by example and daily intercourse with them, and direct chiefly by His example and by opening to them the meaning of the Scriptures. Our Lord, of course, as God knew all things, but in addition, in His human nature, He enjoyed the "Beatific Vision" and possessed "Infused Knowledge," by which He knew all things past, present and to come, without any need of human knowledge, which concerned His mission on earth, and all that was contained in the Scriptures concerning Him. He had no need of acquired knowledge to understand all such things which the ordinary man has to learn by human effort. But it was possible for Him to acquire by human means what He already knew otherwise. Thus He could acquire a knowledge of the Scriptures by study and instruction from others, and so give us an example of application and intellectual activity. But, as we know from His life and teachings, there was much, such as a detailed knowledge of the future, which could not be learned from an ordinary knowledge of the Scriptures. We must, then, in describing—or trying to appreciate— our Lord's acquired knowledge, keep in mind that He had no need of that kind of knowledge, and if He did choose to use His natural faculties, it was because He was "like to us" in His human life, and wished to give us an example of the activities proper to human life. When, for example, we say that Christ "knew Greek" we may not exclude the fact that He had no need to acquire it, but that He also knew it as one who learnt it, and hence conclude His contact with those who knew it. We must keep this in mind when reading such passages as the following remarks of Edersheim on our Lord's knowledge of the Bible:

"Fain would we know it, whether the Child Jesus frequented the Synagogue School; who was His teacher, and who those who sat beside Him on the ground, earnestly gazing on the face of Him who repeated the sacrificial ordinances in the Book of Leviticus, that were all to be fulfilled in Him. But it is all 'a mystery of Godliness.' We do not even know quite certainly whether the school-system had, at that time,

extended to far-off Nazareth; nor whether the order and method which have been described were universally observed at the time. In all probability, however, there were such schools at Nazareth, and, if so, the Child Saviour would conform to the general practice of attendance. We may thus, still with deepest reverence, think of Him as learning His earliest lessons from the Book of Leviticus. Learned Rabbis there were not at Nazareth—either then or afterwards. He would attend the Synagogues, where Moses and prophets were read and, as afterwards by Himself, occasional addresses delivered. That His was a pious home in the highest sense, it seems almost irreverent to say. From His intimate familiarity with Holy Scripture, in its every detail, we may be allowed to infer that the home of Nazareth, however humble, possessed a precious copy of the Sacred Volume in its entirety. At any rate, we know that from earliest childhood it must have formed the meat and drink of the God-Man. . . .

"As we gaze into the vast glory of meaning which He opens to us; follow the shining track of heavenward living to which He points; behold the lines of symbol, type, and prediction converging in the grand unity of that Kingdom which became reality in Him; or listen as, alternately, some question of His seems to rive the darkness, as with a flash of sudden light, or some sweet promise of old to lull the storm, some earnest lesson to quiet the tossing waves—we catch faint, it may be far-off glimpses of how, in that early Child-life, when the Holy Scriptures were His special study, He must have read them, and what thoughts must have been kindled by their light. And thus better than before can we understand it: 'And the Child grew, and waxed strong in spirit, filled with wisdom, and the grace of God was upon him' " (Vol. I, Bk. II, Ch. IX).

We do not need to speculate on our Lord's wonderful knowledge and understanding of the Holy Scriptures, for St. Luke, in his account of Christ's appearing to the two disciples on their way to Emmaus on the first Easter morning, tells how:

"Beginning at Moses and all the prophets, he expounded to them in all the Scriptures the things that were concerning him. . . .

"And they said one to the other: Was not our heart burning within us, whilst he spoke in the way, and opened to us the Scriptures?" (Luke xxiv, 25-32).

We have already seen that both Mary and Joseph were well acquainted with the Holy Book, and were therefore apt pupils for the deeper and wider understanding which Jesus would unfold to them. For we cannot doubt that Jesus opened the Scriptures to them as to no others. We like to think of Jesus reading and explaining the Holy Scriptures to Mary and Joseph on the Sabbath day of rest, and in the quiet of evening in their home, or, as night drew on, without need of parchment roll, telling them how all was to be fulfilled in Him. If our Lord thought it right to prepare His apostles for His passion and the sufferings that were in store for them, it is hardly credible that He would not have prepared Mary, at least in a general way, for her part. If the words spoken by Him when reference was made to her, and which have appeared to some as showing a certain want of affection, are examined in the light of Mary's realisation of the share she was destined to have in His devotion to the will of God, they are more easily explained. It would thus seem to be more than mere speculation to hold that during these hidden years Jesus unfolded to Mary and Joseph "in all the Scriptures the things that were concerning him." Would not their hearts be burning within them at the thought of their—and especially Mary's— association with Him in the magnificent mission which was His? That Mary understood more fully the words spoken by her Son at the marriage in Cana than those spoken by Him in the early days is shown by her whole action. There is no longer any indication of "wonder" or "not understanding" the reply of Jesus, which commentators find so difficult. A perfect understanding had been reached between her soul and His.

Joseph too would have understood better, as the years passed on, his place in the great work of redemption; but his was a hidden part. It is probable that among the portions of Scripture expounded by Jesus was the similarity of his own place in the New Testament with that of the other Joseph in the Old. Several of the Fathers have dwelt on this subject. For example, St. Bernard, in his second homily on *Missus est*, which is read in the Office for the Feast of St. Joseph, says:

"Who and what kind of man was the blessed Joseph may be gathered from the title by which,

although but by privilege only, he deserved to be so
honoured as to be called and believed to be the father
of God; you may rightly gather it from his very name,
which signifies 'increase.' And, while thinking of him,
bear in mind that great man, the Patriarch of old
who was sold into Egypt; and know that St. Joseph
not only inherited his name but was like to him in
chastity, innocence and grace. For if that Joseph, sold
through the envy of his brethren, and carried into
Egypt, prefigured the selling of Christ; this Joseph
flying from the envy of Herod, carried Christ into
Egypt. That Joseph, keeping faith with his lord, would
have no unlawful intercourse with his lord's lady; this
Joseph, knowing the virginity of his Lady, and being
himself chaste, faithfully guarded the Mother of his
Lord. To the former it was given to understand the
mysteries of dreams, to the latter to understand
and have part in the mysteries of heaven. The first
saved the wheat not for himself, but for the whole
people, the second received the Living Bread from
heaven both for himself and for the whole world.
There is no doubt that a good and holy man was this
Joseph to whom the Mother of the Saviour was espoused. He was, I say, the good and faithful servant
whom the Lord constituted to be the comforter of His
Mother, the sustainer of His own body, and finally, as
her sole and most faithful coadjutor on earth in the
great project (of the Incarnation)."

Throughout the Masses and Offices both of the feast
of St. Joseph, and of the solemnity of his Patronage of

the Universal Church, extracts from the history of the
Patriarch are frequently applied to Joseph the husband
of Mary.

Surely there was never man on earth so blessed as
Joseph. Intimate association between those who are
joined together by mutual love and affection is the highest natural happiness and joy which human souls can
know. It would be impertinent to attempt to describe
what this meant in the life of St. Joseph with Jesus and
Mary. But the thought may come that for this very reason Joseph was exempt from that carrying of his cross
which is the lot of all men, for the greater the sanctity
of any child of Eve the greater is the cross to be carried.
Was there any place for suffering in such a life as his?

We have already dwelt on the anxieties, labours and
trials which both Mary and Joseph had to bear, beginning with his anxiety when Mary returned from the Visitation, and the "sorrow" both experienced when the
Child was lost in Jerusalem. If love is the greatest of human joys, it is also of its very nature the occasion of
much suffering. There can be no doubt but that the
greatest suffering of Christ Himself arose from His love
of the Father and of mankind. The dearer the object of
love the greater is the fear of losing it; the closer and
dearer the ties which bind souls together, the greater is
the pain of separation; the purer and more unselfish the
love between souls, the greater is the suffering of each in
the sufferings of the other. Joseph, through the very
depth of his love for Jesus and Mary, was exposed to suffer all these "wounds of love"—to use the words of St.
Francis de Sales. If, as we have every reason to believe,

Joseph knew and realised all that Jesus and Mary were destined to suffer, there was surely enough to place the cross on his shoulder: Mary's heart to be pierced with the sword, and Jesus to be nailed to the cross, and both to suffer more in the other's pain than in their own. But these things are rather to be pondered in our hearts than to put in words.

At the same time, since holy souls, who know that God is with them, are not unduly depressed or horrified by actual or impending evils, we would be wrong to suppose that there was not intense happiness and human joy in the home life of the Holy Family. That family was to be the model of every Christian household, and any interpretation which would represent its members as constantly living under the gloom of impending sorrow would be false to the instincts of the human mind and heart. Rather we picture to ourselves their lives as being full of peace and happiness, taking the great gifts they had received from the hand of God, a life sanctified by prayer, charity and work, each of them knowing that when God sends suffering He never fails to send with it strength, courage and consolation.

Their lives were full of the ordinary human interests arising out of their intercourse with others. They had many relatives in Nazareth with whom they would have had social intercourse, sharing with them their joys and sorrows, and we may be sure Mary would have been in all things the comfortress of the afflicted and health of the weak. The ordinary interest of their work would have brought Jesus and Joseph into contact with all sorts of men, and given our Lord that acquired knowledge of human nature which appears from the Gospels. Then there were the journeys to Jerusalem at different seasons of the year to interrupt their daily round of toil. We would like to know if, during these years, they visited other towns and villages in the country around, but the Gospel is silent on suchlike matters. The one thing we may be sure of is that for all who came in contact with them they were a source of happiness and holiness.

Thus from the meagre details afforded by the Gospel story we can in some such way help ourselves to picture the hidden lives of Jesus, Mary and Joseph. Brief as has been the attempt to describe that life, the thought comes that it were better to copy the reticence of the Gospel and, like Mary, "ponder it in our hearts."

CHAPTER XV

THE DEATH OF JOSEPH

"Blessed are the dead who die in the Lord." (Apoc. xiv, 13).

It is agreed by the vast majority of writers and commentators that Joseph died during the hidden life at Nazareth. The Gospel gives us no direct information as to where or when this great sorrow came to Jesus and Mary. That it was a sorrow needs no proof, and it would be presumptuous to attempt to describe their feelings. We can, however, obtain some indication from the Gospels that Joseph had passed away before the public life of Christ. Our Lady, on more than one occasion, is mentioned as being among those who were with Him, which would seem to indicate that she no longer lived at Nazareth, where she would have stayed had Joseph been alive, for there is no mention of his ever being in company with her or with Jesus. When Jesus preached at Nazareth, St. Mark says that His disciples, in their astonishment at His wisdom, cried out: "Is not this the carpenter, the son of Mary . . .?" (vi, 3). Some commentators take this as an indication that Joseph was no longer living. But, referring probably to the same occasion, St. Matthew reports them as saying: "Is not this

the carpenter's son? is not his mother called Mary?
. . ." (xiii, 55); and St. John tells us that, much later, the
people of Capharnaum cried out: "Is not this Jesus the
son of Joseph, whose father and mother we know?" (vi,
42). It seems clear that from these three versions it is
impossible to deduce definitely whether Joseph was living at the time or not. We may, however, deduce from
the words of St. John describing the death of Christ, that
Joseph was then no longer living: "When Jesus therefore had seen his mother and the disciple standing,
whom he loved, he said to his mother: Woman behold
thy son. After that he saith to the disciple: Behold thy
mother. And from that hour the disciple took her to his
own" (xix, 26, 27).

The only other mention of Joseph is when, at the
baptism of Christ, St. Luke says: "And Jesus himself
was beginning about the age of thirty years: being (as it
was supposed) the Son of Joseph, who was of Heli . . ."
(iii, 23); and "Philip findeth Nathanæl, and saith to
him: We have found him of whom Moses in the law and
the prophets did write, Jesus the son of Joseph of Nazareth" (John i, 45). It is clear that this reference gives
us no information as to the time and place of the death
of Joseph, nor any indication as to whether he was then
living or not.

It is, however, generally agreed that Joseph lived for
some years into the hidden life of Jesus. Suarez deduces
from the words: "And he was subject to them," that
Joseph lived for some years after the return to Nazareth
when our Lord was twelve years old: "This implies that
Joseph lived with them both for some years, almost up

to the years of the preaching of Christ, in order that by his labour he might support Him along with the Virgin."

But the fact remains that we are told nothing at all about the death of Joseph. We may be certain that this was a happy, peaceful death. The tradition of the Catholic Church has always looked on him as the patron of a happy death. Any description of the parting scene would be but imaginary, and the feelings of these holiest of souls had best be left to our own hearts. We like to think—can we not be sure?—that when the time of Joseph's death came, his last moments were consoled by the certain knowledge that Mary and "their Son" would once more be united with him in the kingdom of their Heavenly Father. As he died in their embrace, and looked with love, for the last time, on her who was his dear companion throughout his life, his heart must have been filled with gratitude to God who had joined his life with hers, of whom every fibre of his being echoed the words of the inspired writer, so often applied by the Church to Mary:

"Her have I loved and have sought out from my youth, and have desired to take her for my spouse and I became a lover of her beauty. She glorified her nobility by being conversant with God; yea and the lord of all things hath loved her. For she it is that teacheth the knowledge of God, and is the chooser of his works. . . . And I preferred her before kingdoms and thrones and esteemed riches nothing in comparison of her. I loved her above health and beauty, and chose to have her instead of light; for her light cannot be put out. Now all good things came to me together with her, and innumerable riches through her hands" (Wisdom, viii, 2-4; vii, 8-11).

ST. JOSEPH, PATRON OF A HAPPY DEATH, PRAY FOR US.

SELF-DISCIPLINE
and
THE INTERIOR LIFE

By
DOM IDESBALD RYELANDT, O.S.B.
Prior of Glenstal

Translated by
DOM MATTHEW DILLON, O.S.B.
Monk of Glenstal

A *Selection of*
SPIRITUAL BOOK ASSOCIATES

printed with the permission of
BROWNE AND NOLAN LIMITED
THE RICHVIEW PRESS, DUBLIN

Imprimi potest:
    IDESBALDUS RYELANDT
       Prior

Glenstal, 20° Julii, 1945

Nihil Obstat:
    JOANNES KELLY
       Censor Theol. Deput

Imprimi potest:
    ✠ JOANNES CAROLUS
       Archiep. Dublinen.
       Hiberniae Primas

Dublini, die 16° Novembris, 1945

CONTENTS

INTRODUCTION

WE can all realise how important it is to maintain a certain poise or calm of soul in the ups and downs of life.

This inner peace is achieved largely through the practice of patience and by a wise, calm reaction against one's own natural weakness.

We have to teach ourselves how to react in this way. Making all allowances for the limitations which exhaustion, sickness or natural disposition may impose on our will power, we maintain that we can all do a great deal to develop in ourselves this habit of self-domination or moral reaction.

There are many souls who are too ready to let themselves be carried along by the current of life; they make little or no effort to react against their impressions, their impulses and vexations, their vain desires, against the great troubles of life or the little annoyances which are bound to arise in our daily relations with others. In family life especially this self-control must be strictly exercised to prevent any friction which might trouble the domestic peace. Sulkiness, depression, outbursts of temper and carping criticism must be sedulously avoided in the home if we are to maintain that family atmosphere which gives the home its true dignity.

The man who is a victim of depression finds his power of reaction weakened and his peace of soul is so much the less secure. A word, a gesture, a mere nothing suffices to fan into new life this sadness which obsesses him, to awaken some suspicion, to revive that uncertainty and anxiety which are the characteristics of the scrupulous soul, or those groundless fears which rob the nervous man of his ease of speech or movement.

Whether he suffers from depression or not every man owes it to himself to foster his faculty of healthy reaction. There are many elements from within and without which are hostile to the spirit of duty, to the joy of labour, to the calm of life. We must be able to fight boldly and wisely against all of these if we would maintain our peace of soul.

The faculty of reacting against these difficulties requires prudent development and the educationalist must exercise every care to teach and encourage it in those entrusted to his charge.

This faculty has its place also in the religious life. It counts for a great deal in the daily pursuit of perfection to be able to maintain this balance of soul, this calm, and this universal fidelty. Every age finds its own special difficulties in community life, governed by obedience; and this calm self-control, practised constantly and in a supernatural spirit, is absolutely necessary if we are to overcome them. There is a strong presumption, if not an absolute certainty, that a novice who has not got this self-control and this capacity to react against his natural tendencies has not a true vocation to the religious life.

There are those who are temperamentally inclined to extremes and this is a danger which must be guarded against. This power of reacting must be held in check if it is to have its full salutary effect. The tendency to lean always to the other extreme, though it can be understood in the enthusiasm of youth, is a defect which should be curbed in more mature souls.

Allowance must be made for the capacity of the individual to bear the nervous strain which this effort requires. To react too violently against one's natural dispositions may upset the soul and overthrow the equilibrium which it is sought to establish. In a word, this self-control, to be really beneficial, must be moderate, wise and within such limits as to make it possible to keep up the effort and maintain normal life.

There are five principal sources of moral strength which are at the disposal of every man: each of them in its own way arouses, stimulates and maintains in the soul this capacity to rise above the natural tendencies of the individual character. These are: (1) A sound philosophy of life or, in other words, sound common sense; (2) The spirit of Faith which is the source of the spirit of prayer; (3) Charity; (4) The Blessed Eucharist; (5) Work.

It is intended to explain in this little book the practical utility of these five sources. We do not claim to set out anything which is new, but in the practical difficulties of life we are too often inclined to lose sight of the commonplace truths and these are not the least important.

CHAPTER I

SPIRITUAL BALANCE AND A PHILOSOPHY
OF LIFE

THE conception which every man forms for himself of personal happiness and of the possibility of attaining it has an important influence on his moral balance. Men cause much suffering to themselves and to those around them by their failure to react against unreal and elusive ideas of happiness. Happiness is possible in this world certainly; but it is a qualified happiness mingled with many ills, limited in a hundred ways. It is impossible for man in this world to attain complete contentment, to achieve that fulness of joy which will fulfil all the multiple aspirations of his nature. Even though we had all that health, fortune, talents, learning and friendship could give us, there would always be something to displease us. Our nature is too complex and its needs and desires too contradictory for any combination of circumstances to give us all that we desire.

We must not therefore deceive ourselves by expecting perfect contentment; we must not ask of life a greater measure of happiness than it is capable of giving. In the married state, as in the religious life and in the life of a priest true happiness is certainly to be found, but it must be purchased at the price of a generous reaction against circumstances and it will be mingled with many troubles.

We must appreciate the measure of happiness that is offered to us however modest it may be. Many men allow themselves to be obsessed by gloomy preoccupations. They do not estimate at its true value the happiness that is theirs; failing to recognise the elements which make it up they derive no pleasure from them. By thinking of what we lack we fail to appreciate what we have. Some again will allow the prospect of future ills—many of them may never come to pass—to overshadow the joys of the present. In this way the daily burden of sorrow is greatly aggravated. By failing to appreciate the benefits which God bestows on us at every moment and to thank Him for them, man lessens his capacity for happiness. By failing to exercise his judgment and to react against useless worries, he allows them to spoil that modest happiness which he should enjoy.

II.—The realisation that strife is a necessary element of our life is in itself a help and an encouragement to respond readily to the call of each day on our generosity. In life good and evil are woven together in a pattern which is often complex. We have to choose between the bad, the less bad and the tolerable on the one hand, and the good, the better and the best on the other; and the choice, if it be well made, always requires an effort and a certain generosity. In every domain—be it social, technical, scientific or artistic and above all in the moral sphere—progress can only be achieved by effort. Normally this progress will be achieved in stages and this supposes a succession of efforts followed by partial victories. To attain the heights we must, like the mountain-climber, advance step by step.

If we would avoid failure we must resign ourselves to constant strife and unremitting effort. The history of the Church and its dogmas, the lives of the saints and indeed the story of all the greatest deeds of men afford ample proof of this truth.

The powers of evil are so great and their faculty of regaining lost ground so formidable that no institution, however perfect, can dispense with periodic review and adaptation to changing circumstances.

This applies to the moral effort of every individual: we must resign ourselves to the painful necessity of constant effort. It is the price of merit. We must never lose heart. God in his wisdom has ordained that it should be so. It seems that everything would be easy if the tares were not mixed with the corn. But if there were no injustices, no trials, no sorrows, no opportunity for sacrifice, our virtues would have little scope. We should have no opportunity to prepare ourselves for our heavenly destiny. It would be hard indeed to develop the beauty of our souls in a world where there was no place for effort or heroism.

The surmounting of obstacle and steadfast persistence in the pursuit of good, are essential conditions of all real virtue. In moments of difficulty we should be encouraged by the thought of the multitudes of our fellow-men who are suffering, enduring and striving in face of difficulties much greater than ours. Their abnegation must be our inspiration.

We may learn also from our own past life. We can recall the sufferings which we have endured in the past and how we overcame them. Our triumphs in the past are a pledge of success in the difficulties of the present.

In the battle against our own faults or against those of others we must not forget the words of St. Paul: "Overcome evil by good"—*vince in bono malum*.[1] This counsel is of great importance in all moral training. If we merely try to conquer the evil thoughts that come to us we shall not effect a real cure. It is rather by arousing in the soul an attraction for the good opposed to these inclinations that we can really destroy them by implanting the corresponding virtue. We can conquer laziness more effectively by fostering an interest in some special work than by merely repressing the weakness; the surest way to overcome egoism is to encourage loyalty in some particular form. In practice however neither method of fighting against moral defects excludes the other. Both must be employed according to the circumstances.

III.—There is another truth which should help us to overcome our spiritual difficulties and to react prudently in face of them: it is the simple fact that man consists of matter and spirit, of soul and body.

As a spirit man is certainly immortal, endowed with the divine life and seeks God as his last end; but his spirit does not cease to be connected with matter and we must always reckon with this material influence. Even when

[1] Rom., xii. 21.

exercising his most spiritual activities as thinking, willing, praying or loving God, the soul is dependent on the
brain and on the whole physical organism. Now these
sensible faculties have a privileged position as the soul is
dependent on them and they frequently abuse this privilege. By exaggerating, by false associations, by confusing
the issue, the imagination can raise up false impressions
by which it confuses the judgement and leads it astray.
The different emotions also have their influence on our
sensibility and can control our will. Our nerves, and our
state of health play their part too in influencing the spiritual side. Even in insanity it is not the soul which is
affected but its instrument, the brain, which is dis-
ordered.

We must learn therefore to use our senses and to avail
of the great wealth of information which they provide;
but we must learn also to watch for and prevent the first
beginnings of their encroachments on the spiritual
sphere. Our philosophy of life should teach us not to be
shocked at our own tendencies to evil, nor shrink from
the effort which is incumbent on us to resist them. In
times of emotional stress we must not be troubled by
the extravagances of our imagination, nor by the limitations of our physical and moral strength. To admit discouragement would avail us nothing. We should rather,
in the true spirit of humility, accept the fact of our own
littleness and strive boldly to overcome our weakness according to the true moral ideal which we have set before
us.

The value of our soul in the eyes of God does not depend on our playing the rôle of an incorporeal angel. He asks us rather to accept our nature as it is, in the spirit of love, and to offer it to Him rectified to the best of our ability according to His wisdom and His will.

CHAPTER II

FAITH INFUSING NEW VALUE
INTO HUMAN EFFORT

IF we consider life from the viewpoint of faith we find
our power of self-government immensely strengthened.
The appreciation of the glorious truths which Christianity presents to us and the realisation of the infinite
value of the reward which is at stake give a tremendous
incentive to this inner force of resistance.

If we believe in God as the just judge of all our
actions, listening sympathetically to every prayer, if we
are assured of the possibility of union with the divinity
in Jesus Christ, and of the existence of heaven and hell,
all these convictions based on a living faith make us
realise that our efforts are never sterile but infinitely well
worth the courage which they require.

If we reflect on it we must be struck by the fact that
Christianity in all its complexity is essentially a religion
of optimism at once intense and sincere. Joy is the dominant note: the joy of our charity towards our neighbour,
the joy of hope and the joy of communion with God.
For the believer, for the Christian, the "principle of con-
servation" remains unquestioned, but it is applied in the
realm of moral and religious values. In the eyes of God

nothing is lost. The merit of every good act endures for ever: the Lord contemplates and preserves it in the storehouse of eternity.

We cannot overlook the sad catalogue of human suffering, but in the wide Christian conception of life, pain, work, sorrow, even death itself has its place and contributes to the final good.

The gospel does not overlook the problem of suffering. It faces it squarely. Is it not a part of the mission of Christ and of His Church to comfort human misery, to teach men to accept it and to react to it in the right way?

Laborious effort, sorrow in all its forms, work and even death are raised by the Christian faith to a supernatural plane and given a supernatural value. To the man of faith no human misery is destined to be fruitless or sterile: each one has its place in the designs of Providence. He sees in every trouble an opportunity to purify his soul, to rise to a higher spiritual level or to emancipate himself from the bonds of his lower nature. In the wisdom of God pain may serve, now to expiate for the sins of the past, now to free the spirit of its illusions or liberate the heart from the shackles which are holding it back from the heights to which He has destined it. Often it is the troubles of life which serve to strengthen the bonds of love between Christ and man. There is a reciprocity of love which only finds its true expression on the cross. Grace and high spiritual aspirations are born and developed in our souls most often through some suffering or some disillusionment.

The eyes of faith see in the law of effort proper to this

life no reason for revolt or discouragement but rather a providential opportunity for spiritual growth, for spiritual freedom, for the gaining of our salvation.

If we read again the Beatitudes or the words of Christ after the washing of the feet at the Last Supper we shall appreciate more fully how the Christian idea without eliminating suffering gives it a new meaning at once sanctifying and satisfying. Under the guidance of our faith our power of facing and dominating life without being overwhelmed by it is immensely increased. Lastly, faith, through the value which it attributes to effort and to suffering is our supreme inspiration in the battle against human pride and the egoism of the senses.

II.—This effort must always be sustained by prayer. Prayer is, as it were, its faithful lieutenant. It alone can prevent the soul from lapsing into complacency in the nobility of its own effort. The pagan stoic relies exclusively on the force of his own will to sustain his constancy. He prides himself on his self-sufficiency. The consciousness of his dignity and of his superiority over the common herd is his sole support.

For us however, every effort, every striving towards good requires the help of prayer and consequently the help of God and His grace. Here is the source of that humility which is required of every Christian, even, indeed above all, in the hour of heroism, for he knows that the strength of his will and the noble aspirations of his soul come to him from God alone.

When we have to reprove evil and especially when we have to condemn sin in others we must retain our hu-

mility and our benevolence for the sinner. We must remember that we too are fragile and capable of grave falls
from virtue although we have been preserved by God's
grace. Without it might not we too have erred and fallen
perhaps more gravely than those whose fault we are
judging?

We must appreciate the great resources of moral
strength inspired in us by the convictions of our faith.
St. Paul, writing to the Romans, speaks of the Gospel
as the "power of salvation"—*virtus ad salutem*. Now that
power of redemption which is the property of faith in
Christ is as strong to-day as it was twenty centuries ago;
coming as it does from God and His Love, it is not weakened by the passage of time.

We must adhere firmly to our religious beliefs; we
must vivify them by our spiritual reading, by our meditation and by that life-giving contact with the mysteries
of Christ which is afforded us each year in the liturgy.
In this way we shall learn to appreciate more fully the
rôle ordained by Providence for suffering and effort in
the mystery of our life on this earth.

CHAPTER III

CHARITY: THE INSPIRATION
OF HUMAN EFFORT

MORE even than good sense, more than the spirit of faith, love is an abundant source of spiritual strength. "Love," says the *Imitation*, "is the great good; it alone makes every burden light and every constraint bearable." [1]

I.—Even outside the religious domain this dominant power of love may be observed. When, amidst all the mediocrity and pettiness of life one meets some real act of devotion, a true spirit of sacrifice or of reaction against the intensity of egoism, one is sure to find some great love as its inspiration. It may be the love of a parent for a child, the affection of a sister or a friend or perhaps the simple loyalty of two fellow-workers or comrades-in-arms; it is always charity in some form which inspires man to strive without counting the cost, without flagging in the face of difficulty, for the good of his fellow-men.

If it is so in the order of Nature all the more may we expect that the love of God and the charity of Christ will equip the human will even more fully with the energy for unselfish effort and self-sacrifice. To love is to want God to form a part of our life, to wish to have a part in His goodness, to accept freely His will in our

[1] *Imitation of Christ*, III, v.

regard and to offer to Him the homage of our being and
of our activity.

It is the same with regard to Christ. To love Him is to
keep His commandments, especially the commandment
of charity towards our neighbour; it is to adhere to Him,
the Way, the Life and the Truth, Who is at once High-
Priest and Sacrifice, King and Friend.

In the history of souls this charity has produced the
most sublime effects. From the love of the Apostles and
the holy women for Christ down to the charity of the
most recently canonised saint, the annals of the Church
present a wonderful picture of the degree of heroism, forgetfulness of self and loyalty to which weak human nature can rise under the sanctifying and strengthening influence of Divine Charity.

II.—It may well be that in us, unlike the saints, the
love of God is not always active, always vigorous; it will
not therefore produce in us the same vital power of elevation and of reaction. All the same we must appreciate
this love at its true value and the spiritual energy with
which it endows us.[2] We must fan it into flame.

[2] St. Thomas tells us that Charity requires us to love in ourselves and
in others the act of Divine love itself: *Caritas ex caritate est diligenda*
(*Summa Ia IIae q. xxv, a. 2*). To help us react against our own apathy
it is useful to appreciate that it is right to approve the perfection of this
union with God and the joy which it inspires, to take pleasure in the
generosity of our act of oblation to God and of submission to Him. But,
while approving these acts of charity we must look on them as the ideal
way to love God because He is good in Himself and to offer Him our
existence and our life as an act of disinterested adoration. In our prayer
therefore we may love our act of union in all the fulness of its joy, but
it must be appreciated above all as the means of referring ourselves
completely to God for His own sake. St. Augustine, mindful of these
two aspects of Charity, defined it thus: "The movement of the soul

It is unnecessary to analyse in detail how each of the different forms of Divine Charity may become a source of spiritual strength. We shall take one form of charity which is especially easy for every man to practise and which involves no danger of illusion or of religious sentimentality. Children and grown men, the educated and the uneducated alike can practise this form of charity. I refer to gratitude to God for all that He has given us— a duty which the Church tells us is at all times and in all places just and salutary: *semper et ubique gratias agere.*

This spirit of gratitude not merely consecrates the heart to the duty of homage towards God but, inclining us to frequent acts of thanksgiving, it prepares us to make the necessary moral effort when the occasion demands. There are three defects—which may be well countered by this spirit of gratitude. They are: spiritual indifference or forgetfulness of God, obstinate self-love and lack of control of the senses.

III.—If we want to cultivate this spirit of gratitude we must first react against this evil of religious indifference or forgetfulness of God. Gratitude keeps alive in us the thought of the Saviour, of His condescension for us, of His precepts and His judgments. St. Benedict bases the whole spiritual life on this constant mindfulness of God. He wants us to be "mindful always" *memor sit semper;* to "avoid all forgetfulness" *oblivionem omnino fugiat.* We have all to fight against this spiritual torpor. Such is our human nature: we lose sight of the supernatural

seeking the enjoyment (or the possession of God) for His own sake."— *Motus animi ad fruendum Deo propter Ipsum.* (*De Doctrine Christiana* III. 10.)

side, we become estranged from that atmosphere of love and confidence which is an essential element of the Christian life. We do not appreciate as we should the divine values.

The habit of gratitude constitutes a practical method of reacting against this forgetting of the supernatural. By frequently raising up our hearts in the spirit of gratitude we give new life to our faith in God, in His providence and in our own sublime destiny; the act of thanksgiving stimulates us to a new appreciation of the gift of Christ, of the gift of the Eucharist; it reminds us of the favours which have been showered on us, of the pardon of our offences which has been accorded us; of the immense benefits which we have received through Divine grace. In times of trial and in the hour of prosperity alike, the enthusiasm of gratitude prevents the work, the suffering and all the trifles of life from absorbing us.

In a word, gratitude by the spontaneousness of its movement towards God as the source of all good is a powerful antidote to spiritual indifference, to the forgetting of the divine, and to religious sloth in all its forms.

IV.—Self-love also is overcome by this habit of thankfulness. Self-love finds food for its vanity in everything. Whatever be the nature of our activity, however good our original intention may be, self-love is an enemy harassing us from within. Without depriving our good actions of all merit it inevitably taints them with a certain imperfection. One man feels that he has a certain manual skill, another is a capable scholar, a third is a judge of men. One man has initiative and administrative ability, another has capacity to carry out the work already initiated. Whether it be in recollection and prayer or in zeal and charity the gifts of God are many and diverse. Now in all these departments no one can pride himself on being free from all suggestions of self-love. We must always humbly recognise the fact that to the legitimate satisfaction in work well done vanity will always add some excessive feeling of self-satisfaction, some immoderate desire of personal aggrandisement, some flavour of illicit ambition.

To free ourselves from these obsessions it is important not to attach undue importance to them. We must rather despise them and oppose to this instinct of vanity the serene, elevating movement of gratitude towards God. We must give thanks to God for every form of activity which He permits us to exercise: every talent which we possess, our capacity, our zeal, every aptitude which is ours are simply so many gifts of God. A practical method of resisting the insidious suggestions of the sin of vanity is to see in the suggestions of our self-love so many occasions for thanksgiving to God.

When some movement of self-love arises in our heart we should not wonder at the wretchedness of our nature but rather turn our mind at once towards God in the spirit of thanksgiving. In this way we shall re-establish the spirit of truth in our hearts and find the inspiration to resist the subtle suggestions of our vanity. "We must attribute to God any good that we may see in ourselves" says St. Benedict, "the evil we must accept as our own responsibility." This is a golden rule.

V.—Self-love manifests itself not only in a temptation to vanity but also in a tendency to unreasonable sorrow. We lose heart, become gloomy, lose all courage in the realisation of our limitations, of our deficiencies, of our incompetence. Instead of looking at the bright side of life we dissipate our energy in idle regrets.

Here again gratitude towards God is the sovereign remedy.

If we are overwhelmed by the sense of our own inferiority, if we are troubled by the feeling that we are less generously endowed than others in the goods of this world, in friendship, in the gifts of nature and of grace, we must find in this sense of inferiority another occasion for realising and appreciating more fully God's bounty to us in the supernatural order.

We must appreciate the resources of our own personality, however modest they may be, and thank God for His benefits, not allowing our defects or our faults to discourage us. A blind man summed up his attitude to life thus: "I can think of God and pray to Him better than people endowed with good sight. I can read the books published for the blind; I thank God for all this and I am not unhappy." Let us take example from this spirit of gratitude which enabled the blind man to rise above the sorrows of life and the petty jealousies which are so common among men. An act of thanksgiving places us in close contact with our own better nature and helps us to take our stand firmly on the side of God.

Furthermore we must believe that the defects from which we suffer may form a part of the divine plan. By minimising our successes, by dimming the glory of our achievements they incite us to further effort; they help us to strive with more zeal, they open our eyes to the falseness of human values and arouse in us a true spirit of generosity. Let us not complain therefore if we suffer from an inferiority complex but react against it and give thanks to God.

VI.—This habit of gratitude proves an excellent weapon against a certain indiscipline of the senses or of the flesh. In the morning, when we waken there is a temptation to prolong our rest; sloth insinuates a distaste for a day which begins so early. To this suggestion of our lower nature we must reply with a prompt move-ment of gratitude: *Deo Gratias*—I give you thanks, O God. I thank you for the gift of a new day in which I have a work to do for you: a Mass to assist at or to cele-brate, the privilege of receiving the Holy Eucharist, my duties to perform in the family circle or elsewhere, my bond of love with God to strengthen, virtues to develop, defects to overcome, the divine praises to express in my heart and with my lips.

This spirit of gratitude, while making us appreciate as Christians the wonderful value of our ordinary daily actions, will help us to overcome more easily the slug-gishness of our lower nature.

The same applies with regard to chastity. To dispel the phantasies of the imagination, unhealthy desires or dangerous memories, we may turn with confidence to this spirit of gratitude. We should remind ourselves of the Divine protection which we have enjoyed in the years which have passed, remembering how we have been preserved and supported in times of difficulty, raised up when we have failed, and led into a holier and higher way of life.

This grateful remembrance of the goodness of God will change our train of thought, it will transport us to an atmosphere far removed from all thoughts of immoderate sensual satisfaction. The very act of giving thanks will free us from the thoughts which obsess us and turn our minds to the contemplation of the divine mercy which has been shown to us through the years.

For the Christian every meal is an occasion for giving thanks to God. We speak of saying Grace. By joining a prayer of gratitude to our meals we raise to a new dignity this commonplace incident of our daily life. The animal is obviously incapable of this concept. Only man can appreciate the goodness and liberality of his Creator in thus providing his sustenance and thank Him for it. This raising of our mind to God may not of itself suffice to obviate all danger of excess at table, but it should recall to the Christian man the order of creation and prevent him from being carried away by the satisfaction of the senses as though that was his true purpose in life.

By saying Grace therefore we react in the spirit of gratitude against the materialism into which it is so easy to lapse when we are satisfying the legitimate needs of our body.

VII.—Love, not of God or of any being in particular, but of a high abstract ideal may also give new strength to our power of reaction. To dedicate oneself to the realisation of an ideal whether it be in the realm of art, of science or of virtue is to free oneself from the pettiness of life, to raise oneself to the sphere of disinterested affection, to strive towards a higher end.

This love for an ideal assumes a practical form often in a devotion to some great and sacred cause of transcendent value to mankind. This devotion presupposes the emancipation of the soul from the bonds of mediocrity and egoism. The alleviation of human suffering, whether physical or moral, the salvation of souls, the good of the Church or of one's country, the preaching of the Faith, these are causes which correspond to the higher aspirations of the human soul.

By adopting such a cause man is consecrating himself to the service of an ideal. This consecration, especially when we are young, develops in us the power to strive and to conquer.

Let us therefore develop in ourselves this spirit of disinterested love under whatever form it may present itself to us. By so doing we shall maintain in full vitality the faculty of effort and self-conquest so necessary if we are to achieve the sanctity which is the goal of the Christian life.

CHAPTER IV

THE EUCHARIST AS A SOURCE
OF MORAL STRENGTH

In the Catholic Church the Eucharist stands out as the principal vital source of Divine help. Whatever the age of him that receives it the Blessed Sacrament is the sovereign remedy for human frailty—"*fortitudo fragilium.*" It is the source of that inner strength whereby we can combat the inconstancy of our will: and the tyranny of our passions. By receiving Holy Communion the Christian maintains his moral life in the way of truth; he can develop his generosity to the point of heroism despite the indifference or ignorance of those with whom he lives. *O Salutaris Hostia . . . da robur, fer auxilium.*

I.—Experience teaches us to distinguish in the Christian life three categories of virtuous acts in which the influence of the Blessed Eucharist is especially pronounced. These are: the carrying out of the duties of our state of life, the practice of chastity according to our condition, the final act of resignation, that is the acceptance of death.

In these three domains human frailty is exposed to many temptations. It may however be asserted with all confidence that for every Christian, whatever may be his age, sex, or way of life, the Eucharist provides inspiration for fortitude in the struggle and for victorious spiritual effort.

Youth and age alike must base every effort towards the higher life on the conscientious fulfilment of the duties of their state, and on a wise observance of the spirit of chastity.

Too much stress cannot be laid on the importance of the Eucharist as the basis of the moral life. The director of souls must insist on this in his guidance, not merely of the young, but of every soul committed to his care. Without it a real elevation of the soul to God is impossible. By its aid we may hope to establish firmly in ourselves the habit of prompt and vigorous reaction against anything calculated to hinder the accomplishment of the duties of our state or the practice of the virtue of chastity according to our vocation—whether it be in family life, at school, in business, in the workshop or elsewhere.

It is perfectly legitimate to receive Holy Communion with the sole intention of obtaining the necessary supernatural help to progress and to overcome our difficulties in these two domains, even though the reception of the Sacred Host arouses no sensible fervour in our heart.

In the Blessed Eucharist we have a hidden source of energy placed at our disposal by the Divine mercy. While the world abandons itself to the fascination of sensual satisfaction the children of the Gospel hand down from generation to generation a great tradition of respect and love for their spirit of duty which will always include a jealous observance of the obligations of chastity. The child, the young man and the married couple appreciate alike the dignity of this virtue and count no effort too great to preserve or, if needs be, to regain it. Unless this virtue is firmly implanted in his heart it is impossible for the Christian, whether married or single, to advance in holiness or even to aspire to the higher life.

The Eucharist is the secret leaven which, operating in our souls from our youth, awakens a true love of this spirit of duty and helps us to bear the constraints and restrictions which it imposes on us. "O admirable mystery," says St. Clement of Alexandria, as early as the second century, "to receive our Saviour, to hide Him within us, to keep Him in our breast so that by His aid we may control the passions of the flesh."

The strength which the Blessed Sacrament communicates is as it were a reserve of supernatural energy infused into the soul. This grace does not dispense us from the effort or the zeal which are indispensable if we are to carry out the duties of our state of life; but it is potent to support, to elevate and to sanctify our good-will. By it we may overcome our own inadequacy and rise above the bounds which our own mediocrity imposes on us.

It is important to note however that this Eucharistic grace of fortitude is not given to us directly; it comes to us through charity. By communicating to us the power to adhere closely to Christ by a fervent act of charity the sacrament endows us at the same time with an inner strength derived from this adherence of love and destined to sustain our effort towards moral rectitude. This grace which is conferred on us by our union with Christ in the Holy Eucharist enables us to respond more faith-

fully to the call of duty, and of the virtues, and to accept more readily all that Divine Providence ordains or permits in our life.

Our act of love in receiving Holy Communion will often come from the intellect and the will rather than from any sensible devotion and the grace of moral fortitude which it bestows on us will operate on the subconscious. We must not wonder at this; faith alone can appreciate the value of the Divine gift.

Finally we must realise that the fact of having given ourselves freely to Christ in the Eucharist constitutes as it were a title in the sight of God to receive from Him the necessary help to do His will in the varying circumstances of our lives.

II.—Important as the Blessed Eucharist is in the temptations of our daily life, its help is still more necessary as we approach Eternity. The Christian has a special need of the support of the grace of Christ when he is facing the mysterious kingdom of Death, and is about to appear before God, his Creator, his Father and his Judge.

Man's natural inclination is to shrink from this encounter with death; he clings to life, not so much because he enjoys it, for it is often hard, but because of his instinctive aversion to the act of dying. It is not easy to meet death well, in the manner and at the time fixed for us by Providence. We need the merciful help offered us from on high to sustain our poor human heart in the anguish of this terrible and inevitable adventure.

The Eucharist brings to every Christian soul in its agony the comfort of the Redemption. Thanks to this supernatural aid the Christian faces calmly the terrors of the mysterious beyond and the inexpressible sorrow of this final separation from all that he holds dear. Uniting himself with Christ, he accepts death and, full of confidence, he allows himself to be taken into the arms of Christ and to be incorporated in Him. In the immense unity of the Mystical Body he dies filled with the hope and peace of one who knows that he is loved and that he is saved.

The heroic death of martyrdom is above all other forms of death that in which the soul has most need of the help and the grace which the Holy Eucharist provides. Fortitude and a generosity at once vigorous and humble are more than ever necessary in face of this supreme test. The Christian teaching of the first centuries, at the time of the Roman persecutions, is clear on this point: the Blessed Eucharist gives supernatural strength to the martyr. "No one can think himself capable of facing martyrdom" says St. Cyprian, "if the Church has not armed him for the combat, for the human soul must flinch if it has not been strengthened and elevated by the Blessed Sacrament." And again: "Let the faithful refresh themselves daily with the Blood of Christ so that they also may have the courage to give their blood for Christ." "If St. Laurence triumphed over his sufferings on the grid," says St. Augustine, "it was because he was strengthened by this food and inspired by this chalice."— *Illa esca saginatus, illo calice ebrius.*

III.—Holy Communion may be received outside of Mass. The Church permits this in order to give every facility for receiving the graces of the sacrament and these graces are fundamentally the same whether they are received during the Holy Sacrifice or apart from it. Nevertheless we should prefer to make our Mass and our Communion a great single act of devotion. Holy Communion is the ideal way to participate in the Mass and to unite the Christian and the Church in the sacrifice of the altar.

Catholic piety involves a reconciliation of two extremes: it is essentially interior, being the habit of adoration in spirit and in truth, but this interior devotion must be born of and developed by the practice of exterior acts—assisting at Mass, receiving the Sacraments, reciting the liturgical offices and vocal prayers approved by the Church. This ritual and these formulas sustain, direct and stimulate the spirit of devotion. By uniting our Mass and our Communion in a single act of worship we arrive at a better understanding of how the Eucharist dominates and gives life and sanctity to our efforts toward holiness.

All the normal activities of a Christian—working, resisting evil, serving our neighbour, praying and even suffering form a part of our offering. The old man and the child, the rich man and the poor man, the priest and the layman, the educated and the uneducated, all have the same duty to direct their actions towards God as the beginning and end of all being. All must sanctify the sum of their activities by the same act—the offering of their daily actions to God. This act of oblation is the easiest method and the one which is most natural to us of learning to give God a part in all our work and in all our efforts, however humble they may be.

By this act of oblation, explicit or implicit, man establishes himself in conformity with the divine plan: he refers his effort to God; he acts in full realisation of his dependence on Him. Man's power to fight against the spirit of materialism on the one hand and the spirit of pride on the other depends on this habit of making every action an act of homage towards God. The man who does not adopt this spirit of oblation loses sight of God as his last end; he cuts himself off from the source of hope and comfort ordained for the Christian in this world.

Now the Mass, every morning in the multitude of our churches through the whole Catholic world, stands forth as a sublime rite of offering and of immolation more acceptable in the sight of God than the Sanctus of His angels. And this mystery of oblation in all its sanctity is close to us; it is within the reach of the most humble, all are invited to it. Everywhere and at every hour the Church renews the sacrifice of the Mass so that all the faithful may learn by virtue of this most sacred rite to offer their lives to God and to make their own the grace of fortitude which flows from it.

The oblation presented before God every morning is primarily the Oblation of Jesus Christ. The mystery of the Cross is renewed on the altar as the propitiatory sacrifice of the redemption is presented anew to the Father, but according to the bloodless rite instituted at the Last Supper and perpetuated in the Mass.

In the Mass the Church offers Christ by the hands of its ministers, but not merely as a passive Victim: it is Christ who offers Himself actively and sacerdotally, "*ut principalis offerens*," as the Council of Trent puts it.

When, by the virtue of Christ, the eternal Pontiff, the priest effects the double transubstantiation, the Saviour, in order to apply to us the fruits of His Passion, rendering Himself present on the altar renews the offering of His Passion and Death of which His sacramental immolation is the perfect reproduction.

The Mass may be said to be a new sacrifice distinct from that of the Cross because it is offered by Christ, now glorious in Heaven, according to a bloodless rite of immolation; but it is the oblation of love and obedience consummated twenty centuries ago by the shedding of His Sacred Blood which is presented anew to the Father by this sacramental act of immolation.

The supreme dignity of the offering made each day in the Mass is therefore in no way opposed to the value of the sacrifice of the Cross, as Luther and Calvin assert. The Mass is not a new source of merit or of satisfaction supplementary to the Sacrifice of Calvary, but in accordance with its Divine institution it renders to God all honour and glory—*omnis honor it gloria*—and applies to the faithful the superabundant fruits of grace, of pardon and of mercy which are derived from the merits and satisfaction of the Cross.

Now according to the mind of the Church the Christian can and should join to this Divine oblation that of his own poor life. However modest may be his effort to

live rightly and in the spirit of charity, that effort should
be offered to God.

Speaking of the mixing of a drop of water with the
wine in the chalice at the Offertory, the Council of Trent
teaches that this rite represents the union of the faithful
with their chief, Christ.

The example of Christ offering Himself to the Father
in every Mass is an invitation to us to imitate His gesture
of donation and of love. By example, as it were, He urges
us to participate in His worship of oblation. "Just as I,
stretched on the Cross, stripped of every possession offered Myself freely—so do you also make an oblation of
yourself at every Mass at which you assist." Christ and
His members, this is the full, complete gift which the
Church wishes to present each day before the throne of
God.

By this participation in the great sacrifice of the
Church the work of the Christian, his fidelity to the
duties of each day and his patient, generous acceptance
of the miseries of life are encouraged, fortified and raised
to a higher plane to become worthy of a heavenly reward.

The rôle of the Mass in the Christian life is therefore
of primary importance. By this sacred rite the whole of
our moral life is raised to a supernatural plane and united
to the oblation of Jesus Christ.

IV.—In order however to perfect this gesture of the
Offertory an immense mystery of love and union must
be accomplished: we must receive on our tongue Christ,
the Victim offered in the Sacrifice; we must enter into

eucharistic communion with this Victim of the Sacrifice
in order to unite ourselves more intimately with the act
of oblation. Let us dwell on this thought: the example
of Christ in the Offertory influences us from without, as
it were, but by Holy Communion the Master dominates
us from within and draws up the soul into Himself. He
effects a higher form of union between Himself and the
soul whereby we share in the very life of the Son of God
and through Him are led to the Father.

When Christ is received sacramentally by a Christian
He takes possession in a fuller sense of a soul already
His and unites it more closely to His own oblation and
to that of His Mystical Body which is being offered
eternally in Him and by Him to the Father.

When speaking of His elevation on the Cross, Christ
said: "When I shall have been raised from the earth, I
shall draw all things to Me."—*Si exaltatus fuero a terra,
omnia traham ad meipsum.* This power of attraction is
always active in the sacred Victim of the Sacrifice. By
constituting Himself the food of our souls, Christ exercises over them this inner power of elevation. By an
ineffable dominion He draws souls to Him, in order to
bring them to the Father by making them share in His
own intimate life.

In His sacramental state Christ is above all a victim.
His whole existence is consecrated to the Father. The
Eucharist in giving to the soul the grace of assimilation
to Christ has the effect of making it like to the Divine
Master in its complete consecration to God.

United, at least intentionally, to the Mass, Communion tends to complete the gesture of oblation made

by the soul at the Offertory. By Holy Communion the Christian is led to understand that he must constitute with Christ the totality of the offering made daily by the Church to God. "By Christ whom she offers," writes St. Augustine, "the Church learns to offer herself" —*Seipsam, per Ipsum, discit offerre.*

The whole moral life and moral effort of the Christian finds therefore in the Mass the source of its energy and of its sanctification, and the fulness of its supernatural beauty.

Holy Communion does not add anything to the Mass, as the Most Rev. Dom B. Capelle remarks: "it is rather the culmination of the sacrifice, a splendid peak of its glory."

V.—We should never forget that the perfect accomplishment of the duties of our state in life, the practice of chastity according to our vocation, and the acceptance in a Christian spirit of suffering and death require Divine assistance. Normally it is in the Mass, by the offering of ourselves and by the reception of the Sacred Host that we shall obtain grace in proportion to the sum of the daily effort required of us.

When we leave the church after receiving Holy Communion we must be able to maintain the atmosphere of oblation in our souls. We must keep the deliberate actions of our day at the level of our offering, of the gift of ourselves made that morning to God. The oblation of ourselves in the Mass must infuse a new spirit even into the most ordinary activities of the day.

Through this consecration of our life to God all the

good actions of the day are united to the liturgical act of oblation: they are the realisation in detail of the complete gift of ourselves which we have made in the morning in union with the oblation of Jesus Christ.

Our sacrifice which we initiate at Mass in the morning is thus continued throughout the day and unites our work and our activities to the sacrifice and to the eternal praise of the Saviour.

Christian energy which is the basis of victorious effort will find therefore its chief source in this supreme liturgical act of humble but intelligent participation in the Mass, with the oblation of ourselves instituted at the Offertory and consummated by Holy Communion.

CHAPTER V

WORK

RETURNING to the natural order, it may be said that work is ordained for man as a law of life. "Thou shalt eat thy bread in the sweat of thy brow." No one may disregard this law with impunity.

The force and the balance of our character depends above all on our generous fidelity to this obligation of work. While idleness weakens the soul, faithful application to work, whether manual or intellectual, strengthens our will and awakens in us a consciousness of our own effectiveness.

Work has been given to man by the Author of his nature as a providential weapon against all that is prejudicial to his moral welfare. By devoting ourselves to work we force ourselves, almost unconsciously, to exercise a certain self-control: work involves normally, not merely the necessary effort, but the control and direction of that effort.

We must realise that every lasting achievement involves a certain suffering. No matter how gifted we are we must, in order to apply ourselves to work, overcome our natural apathy and fight against the temptations of indolence. We must concentrate our energy, physical and mental, on the work we have to do. Work compels us also to make the best use of our capacities, to husband them and to regulate their use. The man who works conscientiously learns to economise his time, to work out in advance the use he will make of it, to carry out his work in the normal course of his daily life without resort to exceptional or unusual expedients. It is at this price that we acquire the true sense of order in every domain of life.

Again application to work may often cause a very useful diversion of our thoughts. There are times in our life when our thoughts may be a source of real harm to the soul. Obsessing the mind they prevent us from adapting ourselves to our present state of life and thus lessen the real value of our personality. By work we free ourselves from depressing memories, from vain sorrow, from tendencies to sentimentality or susceptibility. In times of great stress it is invaluable to be able to modify even in a small measure the trend of the thoughts which oppress us.

Admittedly at all times prayer is the most excellent aid to moral effort but ordinarily we must assist it by application to work.

In times of trial and great interior stress it is by work that man regains possession of himself, overcomes his sense of discouragement and renews his interest in life. It is work rather than distractions and pleasure which is our salvation at such times.

If St. Jerome devoted himself with such zeal to the study of Hebrew it was certainly not because he despised prayer but because he felt the necessity of work the better to counteract the impulses of his difficult character.

Mlle. Legras, the spiritual daughter of St. Vincent de Paul, was a victim to scruples. She aspired nevertheless to a contemplative life. The saint, to free her from the obsession of her thoughts, enjoined her, against her own inclinations, to devote herself to the care of the sick in the hospitals of Paris. By engrossing her in intense work, he cured her and achieved her sanctification by a path other than that which she would have chosen for herself.

St. Benedict in his Rule stresses the importance of work. In doing so his primary intention is certainly to insist on his sons providing for their subsistence in accordance with the law of nature; but he intends also that this daily labour should be a means of combatting all the vices which are inherent to idleness. Idleness not only opens the way to unhealthy desires and futile rivalries, to jealousy and other pettiness of spirit but also develops in the soul a feeling of incapability, and reconciles it to the leading of a useless life. To the idle man life appears to consist of a series of impossibilities. On the other hand, as we have said above, work gives us new life; it stimulates our activity and gives us an intimate conviction of our power to achieve what is good and to resist what is evil.

II.—If we would make our work a source of moral balance we must endow it with certain qualities which will ensure its utility.

First of all we must learn to exercise a certain self-control in our work; that is to say, to accomplish it without feverish agitation or any sacrifice of our inner peace. This practice will permit us to achieve a certain proportion between our effort and the result to be obtained and to preserve order and clearness of purpose in our activity. This self-control will make it easier for us to work in a spirit of recollection, in the presence of God and for His sake. In this way, work will be to us a source of sanctification like a prayer.

III.—For our work to be fruitful we must have, secondly, the spirit of perseverance, and of constancy in our effort. It is a real source of strength not to dissipate our energies in side-issues, to persevere in the same line, to be able to plough to the end the furrow which we have begun. Competence in any domain can only be achieved by a long and faithful application to the same kind of study or work.

Admittedly it is often good to alternate different kinds of work, to vary our occupations. We have no desire to depreciate a general culture. But too much change, a want of constancy in our application is bound to produce a dissipation of thought, dilettantism, a lack of precise knowledge. Work of this kind is of little value in the spiritual life.

IV.—Collaboration is often necessary in an undertaking: Circumstances ordain that one should give his help and the other must be able to welcome and put to good use the effort of his colleague. In these times of individualism the faculty of collaboration with others in a work is not common. Collaboration requires a certain sacrifice of one's own point of view and of one's own manner of working. We have to show consideration for our collaborators in the work and sacrifice something of our personal independence. The man who is availing of the help of another and the man who is giving the help must realise that their task is one of mutual assistance. Some of us are too much inclined to believe in our own self-sufficiency; we take too much on ourselves to the detriment of the work on hand. In practice, we must learn to avail of the help of others in the intellectual as well as in the spiritual domain; we must learn to welcome collaboration, to encourage and make use of the aptitudes of others. We must not seek the glory of individual achievement; let others share in the satisfaction of a work accomplished.

V.—Lastly we must be careful to increase the moral value of our work by supernaturalising our primary intention. The intention which inspires our zeal is of primary importance. We must avoid self-centredness in all its forms; we must know how to share generously in the interests of our neighbour, and give of ourselves for the sake of others. We must not leave all the drudgery to others or seek to avoid our share of the hard work.

We must learn to seek the good, the true and the beautiful for their own sake and for the sake of God who wishes the Christian to rise to a higher spiritual level by his activity. Even the trivial duties of life achieve a certain grandeur when they are accomplished in a disinterested spirit. We must learn to infuse the immensity of charity into the mediocrity of our labours.

By means of this infusion of charity our work is fused with the Divine and acquires an eternal value in the acceptation of God.

If it is endowed with these fundamental qualities work will assure us successful reaction in our spiritual difficulties and a healthy balance in our moral life.

In conclusion we may draw attention to the necessity of distinguishing among the different principles of reaction and of moral balance those which may be of most use to each one of us personally.

Besides the five fundamental sources of moral strength which we have considered, there are others, derived from these, which are at our disposition. To mention a few of these: the examples of duty and of charity furnished by so many heroes unknown to the world at large—the support of friendship in the true sense of the word—discreet spiritual direction—spiritual reading—meditation. At certain moments of life we must avail of all the resources at our disposal if we are to make the necessary effort and maintain our ideal.

Besides all these sources of spiritual balance, prayer in all its forms provides the Christian with invaluable support in his moral effort. Whether it be simple vocal prayer, participation in the liturgical prayer of the Church or contemplative prayer, adhering to God or losing ourselves in Him, it will always infuse into us the spirit of faith and find its consummation in charity and in fidelity to Our Lord.

We must therefore pray frequently and our prayer will assure to the soul interior peace and a life of active submission to God in the spirit of patience and of peace.

At the hour of our death we shall profit by all that we have merited in this world and shall appreciate the value of the treasure of good habits which we have contracted in our earlier life.

When we meditate on this decisive moment, as St. Benedict urges us to do, let us react calmly and prudently against everything that is contrary to rectitude of life, always bearing in mind how infinitely great is the recompense appointed to us for the sacrifices of our life here on earth. Our reward will be God, His love and His Heaven for eternity.